GREEN GUIDE

INSECTS

OF AUSTRALIA

Paul Zborowski

Series Editor: Louise Egerton

First published in 2002 by New Holland Publishers
Sydney

newhollandpublishers.com

A record of this book is held at the National Library of Australia.

ISBN 9781864367379

Series Editor: Louise Egerton
Project Editor: Yani Silvana
Design and Illustrations: Nanette Backhouse
Production Manager: Arlene Gippert
Printed in China

Keep up with Reed New Holland
and New Holland Publishers
NewHollandPublishers
@newhollandpublishers and @ReedNewHolland

Photographic acknowledgements
Photographic positions: t=top, b=bottom, m=main, i=inset

Denis Crawford: p. 37b, p. 76b, p. 90, p. 91m; Mike Cermak: p. 78i;
Scott Ritchie: p. 58b; Owen Kelly: p. 79; CSIRO Entomology: p. 41b, p. 89t, p. 91i

CONTENTS

An Introduction to Insects

Insects are the most successful group of animals on the planet. They can produce many generations in a short time and each individual produces large numbers of offspring every time. Insects are marvellously adapted to all sorts of lifestyles and they have evolved to live in virtually all habitats, from hot springs to snowy mountain tops and the driest of deserts.

What Is An Insect?

Insects are invertebrates. That is, they lack an internal backbone and skeleton. Instead they wear their skeleton on the outside of their body. All the creatures which have this 'exoskeleton' are known collectively as arthropods (from the Greek for 'jointed legs'). Crustaceans, spiders, centipedes and other small creatures share the same strong, waterproof and energy-efficient body design.

The Blue-banded Bee is one of thousands of native bee species in Australia.

Insects evolved from marine crustacean-like creatures with many legs. All insects have three main body parts – head, thorax and abdomen – as well as six legs and two, or occasionally one, pair of wings.

SPIDER SPY

Look closely. If your insect has two main body parts, not three, and eight legs, not six, you've probably got a spider in your sights, not an insect.

Number of Insect Species

There are a lot of insect species in the world. Currently about one million species have been named in scientific collections worldwide, about 80 000 of these in Australia. However, new research suggests that there are vast numbers of new species in the tropics of the world. In some of these areas every tree harbours a suite of insect species unique to that particular tree. The neighbouring tree may shelter another completely different suite of insects. Given this, there may be five to ten million species in existence in our world today.

WORDS TO KNOW

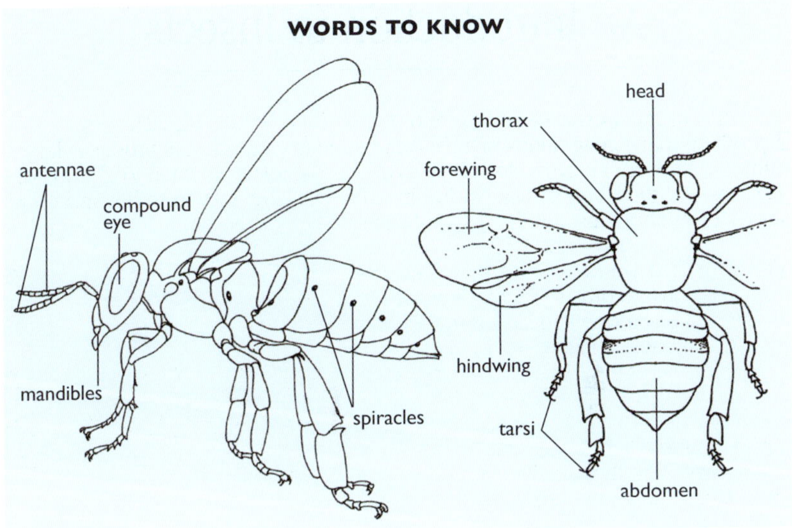

Insect Body Parts

The first part of an insect's body, its head, has one pair of antennae, two compound eyes and mouthparts that either chew sideways, or are modified into sucking (bugs) or mopping (flies) structures. The second part, its thorax, has three segments, each with a pair of legs; one or two with a pair of wings. The top pair sometimes hardens to form a protective wing case. The abdomen forms the third main part of its body. It is divided into 11 segments with the genitals at the end.

Internally the body is almost all one cavity, with a heart running the whole length. There is a stomach near the rear and sometimes an extra stomach, or crop, to carry food to share with others in the nest. Insects have a small brain that is joined to a series of sub-brains called ganglia, which help control functions such as walking, flying and mating. Various glands in the body produce pheromones used to attract mates and for other communication. Insects breathe through spiracles along the sides of the body.

How Do Insects Grow?

The tough, waterproof, jointed exoskeleton of insects is made of layers of a strong plastic-like substance called chitin. This gives maximum strength without weight. The price for this convenient armour is that it cannot grow. It must be replaced every time an immature insect, like a caterpillar, needs to increase its size.

Before shedding the outer skin or 'cuticle', insects produce a new, soft layer underneath it. The hard outer cuticle then splits along most of the body and the insect literally climbs out of its skin. This is called moulting. It then has to pump itself full of air to increase its size before the new cuticle hardens, otherwise the body will not be any bigger after all this effort. On average insects shed their skins about six times in a lifetime before becoming adults. Each stage is called an instar.

The shed exoskeleton of this assassin bug will remain attached to the leaf stem.

What Is Metamorphosis?

Metamorphosis literally means to change form. There are two main types of metamorphosis in the insect world.

In the first, an egg hatches into an immature nymph, which resembles an adult but lacks wings and sexual organs. The nymph grows by shedding its skin 5–10 times until it is an adult. This is called 'incomplete' metamorphosis and is typical of insects like bugs and grasshoppers.

In 'complete' metamorphosis – typical of insects like beetles and butterflies – the egg hatches into a larva, which looks nothing like an adult. Usually a grub-like feeding machine, it lives and feeds exposed on leaves, or hidden in wood or soil. It grows and sheds its skin about five times before entering a pupa stage. The body within the pupa shell transforms into an adult. In the next warm season the adult emerges, often winged, and takes off to seek a mate.

The advantage of complete metamorphosis is that it uses two different habitats and foods in one lifetime, giving these insects a greater chance of survival.

This Leafwing Butterfly is resting on the 'shell' of the pupa from which it has just emerged.

How Long Do Insects Live?

The queens of social insects, like bees, have the longest life spans – 10 or more years for some ants and termites. But while some insects can live many years, others may complete their entire life cycle in as little as a week.

A termite queen dwarfs the size of workers and soldiers, and in one African species has been recorded up to 50 years old!

Perhaps surprisingly the adult, often flying, stage is the shortest period of an insect's life. Indeed, for insects that develop from egg to larva to pupa to adult, like butterflies, most of their life is spent as a larva. For caterpillars it's a matter of weeks; for beetle larvae living in tunnels of wood, a year or two is not unusual.

This difference is due in part to differences in food: caterpillars eat nutritious food like leaves, while beetles feed on wood. Also a long life in the open is not as safe as one hidden in wood. Temperature, too, influences the time insects spend in development. In cold regions or seasons, development slows or stops. Insects living under these conditions often have only one generation a year. Those in the tropics, on the other hand, develop throughout the seasons and can have several generations a year.

THE OLDEST INSECT

The longest lived insect recorded is a beetle in Europe whose larvae were accidentally incorporated into furniture. Fifty-one years later the surprised owners witnessed a tenacious beetle emerging from their furniture. Clearly, the eggs had been laid in a living tree.

Why Are Insects Small?

In sci-fi stories giant insects menace the human race but smallness is a necessary attribute of insects.

For example, an insect's tough waterproof exoskeleton is essentially a cylinder, which is exceedingly strong when small, but would be less so in a bigger animal. An even more important size-limiting factor is their breathing system: they have no lungs or pump like our diaphragm. Instead their bodies are riddled with a mass of tubes called tracheae, which open to the outside via holes called spiracles and allow air to diffuse in and out of the body. They simply can't absorb enough oxygen to grow wider than about 20 mm. Oxygen needs to reach all parts of the body for the insect to live, and if they were any wider it wouldn't reach the middle.

The Goliath Stick Insect can be over 200 mm long but its primitive breathing system helps restrict its width to less than 20 mm.

THE AQUATIC INSECTS

Why Do Some Insects Live in Water?

Underwater drama as a diving beetle devours another predator, a water scorpion.

About 10 per cent of modern insects spend half or all their lives either on or underwater. Most places on Earth can potentially provide food and accommodation for living things but water is quite a benign place for insects to occupy as it is relatively stable. Sudden extremes of weather, like storms and fluctuations in temperature are rare, and water plants grow fairly steadily to form the basis of a reliable food chain.

The crustacean-like ancestors of insects lived in oceans. They used gills to absorb dissolved oxygen from the water. Although modern adult insects have evolved an air-breathing system, many immature stages of insects still have gills. This allows them to live in water and escape from the extreme competition for food and shelter on land. Aquatic insects share the depths with other creatures but the surface of water is a habitat almost exclusively their own. This ability to live *on* water is due to their size and special adaptations (see page 21).

How Can Insects Eat Underwater?

You can't eat a sandwich underwater but an insect could. If we tried, apart from the sandwich being disgustingly soggy, the water would rush into our mouth every time we opened it. It would force its way down our throat and into our lungs. Very soon we would begin to drown. But insects breathe through their spiracles (see page 7) and so they can handle some water entering their mouth with their food without fear of drowning. The spiracles of water insects are usually hidden under the wing cases to stop water rushing in.

A water scorpion sucks the body fluids out of its prey underwater without fear of drowning.

Do Insects Drink?

Insects rarely come down to a creek or puddle for a drink. Probably their main source of free-standing water is dew or rainwater on the surface of plants.

Many insects do not need to seek out water at all as they get sufficient from their food. Caterpillars, for example, generally survive on water from the leaves they munch. Many predators obtain enough fluids from the bodies of their prey. Even in very dry environments, insects can extract some fluids from dried seeds and dead grasses.

A paper wasp collecting water from a bird bath to make the paste for building its paper nest.

Note that mud and paper wasps, which are commonly seen around water, are not looking for a drink: they use the water to bind their nest materials.

FLY FISHING

People who fish in fresh water have been observing the habits of their prey for a very long time, and know of the fondness fish have for insects. The art of fly fishing uses lures designed to mimic flying insects that fall onto the surface. Mayflies are the favourite model as they spend their short adult lives very near water. The lures are often elaborately crafted using feathers around a wire frame.

Are Dragonflies Territorial?

Watching dragonflies go about their business is one of the most rewarding activities when sitting by a creek or pond. The colourful males are very territorial, and guard a stretch of water up to tens of metres long. Males cause near collisions with other intruding males, and two males may spiral upwards in a sparring dance. The ritual can turn nasty, and mid-air fights may end with an intruder plopping onto the water to become instant prey for fish. The less colourful females are welcome in the patch and the males know which ones they have mated with, permitting only those to lay eggs in their territory.

Male dragonflies like to sit at the tips of fine perches to get a better view of the goings-on in their territories.

Dragonflies

A dragonfly literally has eyes in the back of its head.
Inset: Its deadly jaws concealed, a dragonfly larva stalks its prey.

Dragonflies are hunters and use their enormous eyes to search for flying insects in all directions at once. Their four large wings are capable of independent motion, making them the most acrobatic of all flying insects. They can change direction, even from forward to reverse, almost instantaneously. Even flies are not as agile and often end up as a dragonfly's dinner.

Mating and Life Cycle

Males and females hunt separately, coming together near water to mate. Their in-flight mating position is unique; their genitalia meet at the neck and mid-abdomen in a 'wheel' shape. The male, still attached, guards the hovering female as she lays individual eggs onto the water. The eggs eventually sink to the bottom. The larvae, fully aquatic and with gills for breathing, camouflage themselves with algae. Their deadly set of jaws shoot forward to catch prey like tadpoles and other water insects. After a year – or two years in colder parts – the larvae climb out of the water and the flying adults emerge, leaving behind characteristic skins on reeds or trunks.

ANCIENT MONSTERS

The first land insects evolved around 400 million years ago, twice as long ago as the first dinosaurs, and some have hardly changed since. Cockroaches look similar now to how they looked to a *Tyrannosaurus rex*. But at the time that insects invented flight, over 300 million years ago, the largest insect ever was a dragonfly with a wing-span of about 75 cm, wider than that of a magpie. It soared in the great wet forests that became our coal beds.

Mayflies

Three 'tails' and upright wings distinguish a mayfly from other water insects. Inset: Mayfly nymphs have hair-like gills.

Mayflies are related to stoneflies but are easily distinguished by the presence of three long 'tails' called cerci, on a delicate, large-winged body. They are better known in Europe where, in the short summer, many species fill the sky above streams with a spectacular coordinated emergence of the short-lived adults. In the generally warmer Australian climate, emergence is more continuous, with several generations per year in the tropics.

THE SHORTEST LIFE

Mayflies are famous for having apparently very short lives. Adults live only a few days, sometimes just one. Fish feast on the dead swarms floating in mats on the water. However, a mayfly's complete life cycle is not short at all: from egg to adult takes usually one, and up to three, years. An aphid has the shortest insect generation span; it progresses from adult to the next generation adult in just four days.

Mating and Life Cycle

The males come together in flying swarms which attract the females, who enter the fray from above. They mate in flight and lay eggs directly onto the water.

Their aquatic nymphs, famous for moulting up to 50 times, also have the three tails as well as many layers of small, hair-like gills. Most prefer clear streams, where they feed on algae either by scraping it off rocks or by filtering particles from the moving water. Some like very fast waters and attach themselves under rocks using suction pads.

After a year – or two in colder areas – the nymphs emerge and moult into a unique winged pre-adult stage, lasting only minutes to hours. After a further moult the adult emerges. Since it does not feed, its guts are filled with air to make flying easier.

Stoneflies

Unlike mayflies and caddisflies, stoneflies fold their wings close around the body when resting.

Stoneflies are an ancient group of aquatic insects with a flying adult stage similar to that of mayflies. Both have aquatic larvae but, unlike the very short-lived and non-feeding mayfly adults, the mature stoneflies feed and live for up to seven weeks. Also unlike adult mayflies, which hold their wings up high when resting, stoneflies fold their large, membranous wings along the body. Distinguishing them further from mayflies are the two short 'tails'of stoneflies.

Behaviour and Life Cycle

Stoneflies live near water, especially cool, flowing streams. They feed on algae, lichens and rotting wood. After mating the females fly near the water surface and drop in sticky eggs one by one. Up to 1000 eggs drift to the bottom and stick to rocks and plants. Some species venture underwater to lay a single egg mass.

While some larvae breathe by diffusing oxygen directly from the water, most have small tufts of gills on their bodies. They hide beneath stones and feed on algae and detritus. A few species hunt other aquatic insects. In Europe, larvae live up to four years with over 30 instars (stages) but in Australia one to three years is normal, depending on temperature, with 10–14 instars. Adults emerge when the last instar crawls out onto the rocks.

A POLLUTION METER

Scientists use the presence or absence of stoneflies and many species of mayflies as an indicator of water quality. These insects require very well aerated, clean water; if either of these attributes is lost, so are the insects. They live in cool, clear, flowing streams, often high in mountains or on cold southern islands, where they are an important part of the food chain.

Caddisflies

Fluffy caddisfly wings resemble those of moths, to which they are related. Inset: A 'caddis worm' emerges from its glued sand case.

Caddisflies are distantly related to moths. The adults hang about near water and are sometimes confused with stoneflies and mayflies. They differ from these by holding their wings closed in a raised tent-like position, and by not having any 'tails'.

Beautiful Homes

Caddisflies are named after the coarse fabric that was once used for bindings. The fully aquatic larvae, sometimes called caddis worms, are famous for the homes they weave and bind underwater. Most construct elaborate cases, using silk-bound leaves or sticks and other debris. The best sculptors create structures out of sand and pebbles, sometimes perfectly imitating curled snail shells. When moving and feeding, the larvae reach out and drag the case, which is tightly hooked to the tail end.

Behaviour

Most eat plants, detritus, algae and microscopic plankton. Some hunt other aquatic insects and crustaceans. To pupate, the larvae close off the case and sometimes spin a separate cocoon inside. To hatch, the pre-adult stage has to chew its way out of the case and swim to the surface, where it sheds the pupal skin to release the winged adult. Some hatchings are synchronised and produce huge numbers of adults, clouds of which may be attracted to nearby lights. Such big numbers make them an important part of the aquatic food chain.

NET FISHING

Not all caddisfly larvae construct cases out of silk-glued material. One family is famous for spinning flimsy shelters of silk alone. To these are sometimes attached quite elaborate nets which are strung across the current. The nets capture small crustacean and insect prey as it moves downstream.

When Is a Dragon a Damsel?

Dragonflies and damselflies are closely related but do have some obvious differences in form and habits. Dragonflies are generally broader and bigger, and their wide hindwings are larger than their forewings. Damselflies have narrow wings which taper towards the body. When at rest they fold their wings above and along the body, while dragonflies hold them out flat. Their aquatic larvae also differ: damselfly larvae have three big leaf-like gills at their rear end, while the gills of dragonfly larvae are almost invisible. Both stages of both groups are hunters, although the damselfly larvae lack the hinged extension of the jaws which dragonfly larvae shoot forward to surprise their prey. Most ponds will have both flying about in the sun catching insects on the wing.

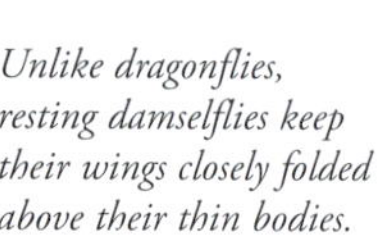

Unlike dragonflies, resting damselflies keep their wings closely folded above their thin bodies.

How Do You Find Aquatic Larvae?

A damselfly larva is quite well camouflaged among vegetation at mid-water, though more stay near the bottom.

The density of aquatic insects in most ponds is surprisingly high. Just run a sieve along the bottom to see how many wriggling forms there are. Don't forget to put them back in the pond so they can continue this life cycle.

The majority of aquatic insect larvae live close to or on the bottom of still waters, such as lakes, ponds and puddles. Few swim about at mid-depth where they are vulnerable to fish, who love to eat their protein-rich bodies. Mayfly, stonefly and caddisfly larvae feed mainly on plant matter gleaned or filtered off algae-covered rocks and litter on the bottom. Dragonfly and damselfly larvae eat these and other insects, so they stay near the bottom, too. Some larvae live long enough to grow a camouflaging layer of algae on their bodies, providing them with added protection. They will remain invisible until they lunge out for the kill.

What Happens When the Pond Dries Up?

Crowded mosquito larvae get the message that the pond is drying, and develop faster, quickly becoming adults which can escape on the wing.

Australia is famous for having the highest river index in the world. This is a measure of the difference between highest and lowest water levels and in this arid continent many water bodies are dry more often than wet.

Aquatic insects use several survival strategies during dry periods. Most have winged adults that simply fly away in search of wetter places. Simple, except that the adult stage represents less than a quarter of the life cycle; the other stages remain stuck in the mud.

Surviving the Dry Times

Eggs of some stoneflies can survive desiccation for 18 months, and the eggs of the pesky desert blackfly can remain viable in deep mud for up to five years. In Africa a midge larva can completely dry out, and in this state of suspended animation called cryptobiosis, it can briefly withstand temperatures of 100°C. Some midges in Australia are known to partly dry out as pupae and survive drought with temperatures up to 57°C. Many larvae that dig into the mud, however, do not survive the drought period.

Another survival strategy is to grow fast. Like some tadpoles, there are water insects that resort to cannibalism during a drought to enrich their diet and finish their growth cycle quicker. The faster growth cycle means the larvae eat less and so grow less, resulting in smaller adults that season, which can leave the pond earlier.

Cast larval skin left by the flying adult dragonfly.

EGG FLOATS

Many aquatic insects simply drop their eggs into water during or after mating flights. Such eggs need to 'breathe' underwater. To avoid this extra complexity, many mosquitoes lay their eggs on the bank or reeds where they will wait for a rise in the water level to hatch. Other clever mosquitoes lay boat-shaped eggs with little air floats. These are joined into 'rafts' that bob on the surface until they hatch.

Fish-killer Bugs

With raptorial legs poised for striking, a fish-killer bug awaits its unsuspecting prey.

These are members of the 'true bugs' (see page 60). Most true bugs are terrestrial but fish-killer bugs are aquatic. They can swim underwater but they spend most of their time hanging upside down from reeds waiting for prey to swim by. Sometimes known as 'giant' fish-killer bugs, they grow to about 8 cm long.

All fish-killer bugs have a flattened boat shape with two pairs of very flat, fringed legs for swimming underwater. The pair of grasping front legs, which look somewhat like ice tongs, have powerful muscles for gripping slippery and strong prey, including fish and frogs larger themselves. Like all true bugs, they stab their prey with mouthparts modified into a sharp syringe-like beak called a rostrum and pump digestive enzymes into their prey to liquefy them before sucking out the contents. Fish-killer bugs hold air for breathing in a space under the wing covers when swimming underwater.

SNORKELLING BUGS

Those adult water insects that lack gills for breathing directly in water normally store air when diving. However, fish-killer bugs and water scorpions have a snorkel-like siphon extending from their rear. This enables them to sit still head down in the water all day, safely hidden among aquatic vegetation. By pumping their abdomen they can also suck in extra air to store under their wing cases for swimming.

Sticky Eggs

Males of some species make low-frequency vibrations on the water surface to attract females. After mating, females of certain species glue their eggs onto the back of the male, where they remain safe for the two-week incubation period. Like all bugs the young, called nymphs, look like wingless versions of the adults and shed their skin about five times to grow.

Diving Beetles

Mid-water reeds provide a good vantage point for ambushers like diving beetles.

BEETLE IN A BUBBLE

Diving beetles carry their own 'aqualung', an air bubble, with them underwater. They back up to the surface to store air under their wing cases where their breathing holes are located. The extra air protrudes as a bubble while they swim, giving them about 20 extra minutes of oxygen. As the oxygen pressure in the bubble gets lower than that in the water around it, oxygen from the water diffuses into the bubble to equalise this pressure, enabling diving beetles to stay down for over a day on a single 'breath'.

There are several families of aquatic beetles but only the fast-swimming hunters are called diving beetles. There are about 180 species, varying in length from 1 to 40 mm. They live in most freshwater bodies, and even in brackish ones.

The smooth, streamlined adults are very hard to hold between your fingers. As they 'row' through the water, a fringe of hair on their hindlegs flattens on the forward stroke and expands on the backstroke, making each movement very efficient. An interesting study found that most species swim at about the same speed but the number of 'oar strokes' changes from 16 per second for little ones to a stately two per second for the largest.

Mating and Life Cycle

Their slippery bodies could make mating difficult but the males have suction pads on their front feet which hold the females underwater. The eggs usually just drop to the bottom.

The larvae are aquatic killers with large jaws. They have as big an appetite as the adults for other water insects, tadpoles and fish, which they hunt with stealth and speed. Unlike the adults, which chew, the larvae suck out their prey through hollow jaws. To pupate, larvae burrow into the wet banks of the pond, from which the flying adults hatch out.

What Bug Swims Upside Down?

Coming up for air, the real backswimmer is the upside-down one; the right-side up one is its reflection.

The aptly named backswimmers are a family of water bugs which spend their lives upside down, and swim a kind of backstroke. Their boat-shaped bodies are convex above and flat below, like an upside-down boat. Very long, oar-like back legs propel them underwater too fast for most predators to keep up. Tiny hairs on their underside capture a layer of air bubbles for breathing, which looks silvery underwater.

They hunt throughout the pond, using their short middle and front legs for grasping insects and small fish. They inject prey with digestive enzymes to liquefy the contents before sucking them out. Their strong beak, called a rostrum, can deliver a painful bite.

Like some other water bugs, males of some species of backswimmers use sound in courtship. They rub their beak with their front legs, making a clicking noise that speeds up to a hum when approaching the female.

What Bug Swims Right Way Up?

The water boatmen are a family of aquatic bugs which look similar to the backswimmers above, but they swim right way up. Their bodies are more flattened, less boat shaped. Their rear legs are long and oar-like. Their thin middle legs are even longer than those of backswimmers and are used to anchor the insect to the bottom of the pond. The very short front legs are equipped with hair-fringed scoops, with which they dig out tiny prey, such as protozoans and small insect larvae, from the bostom of the pond.

They store air under their wing cases and, like backswimmers, also make sounds during courtship. The sounds have been observed to emanate from rubbing together many parts of the body, including the legs, beak-like mouthparts and even the genitalia.

This water boatman is resting near the surface of the pond after collecting air under its wing cases.

Which Insects Walk on Water?

Many insects skate on the surface but the water measurer walks slowly on calm ponds, stalking its prey.

The surface of lakes, rivers and puddles accounts for a lot of area, and nature is not wasteful. The surface tension of water is surprisingly strong, able to support objects heavier than water – try the old school science experiment of placing a steel pin carefully on the surface.

A few spiders are surface-dwellers but over 100 species of bugs live exclusively here. These are the water striders and water measurers. They are mainly hunters, feeding on insects that fall onto the water. The secret that enables them to 'walk' on water is primarily the fine layer of velvety hairs on their 'feet'. Trapped air in the minute spaces between the hairs literally repels water.

WET MOTHS

All insects come from aquatic ancestors. Many modern water insects are land insects that have re-evolved ways of living in water to take advantage of this benign and rich habitat. Moths are the most unexpected insects to return to the water. About 60 species of moths from one family have aquatic caterpillars that build leaf or stone shelters bound with silk, similar to those of caddisfly larvae. They feed on leaves and algae and breathe via thin gills that cover the body like hair. Amazingly the adult moth of one species dives underwater to lay its eggs and then resurfaces and flies away.

Life on the Edge

Other insects, especially beetles, live at the water's edge. Whether they are plant feeders or hunters, they may have to escape predators quickly, either onto the water or back to the shore. A spectacular adaptation for this belongs to a little rove beetle, which can suddenly release an oily fluid from its rear. Upon contact with water the fluid expands, pushing the tiny beetle forward only a small distance but at an amazing rate of up to 150 body lengths per second: this is the equivalent of a dinghy travelling at over 2000 km per hour.

Whirligig Beetles

Whirligigs typically sit half in and half out of the water, observing both worlds. Inset: Underwater, with a sustaining air bubble.

Mobs of whirligigs gyrating madly together on the surface of ponds and streams are a common sight. As well as being entertaining they also possess the most amazing adaptations for a watery life.

Watery Adaptations

The body is very streamlined and produces a water-repelling chemical for extra slipperiness. This, combined with the efficient oar-like design of their short middle and rear legs, makes them the fastest swimming insects. They can attain a speed equivalent to a human swimming 25 km per hour. Their 'oars' have long, flattened hairs which collapse on the forward stroke and expand on the backstroke. Their long, thin front legs are adapted for grasping prey. Each eye is divided in two, making completely separate pairs. One pair watches for airborne attackers, the other surveys the depths for aquatic enemies.

Diet and Behaviour

Adults feed mainly on insects that fall onto the water surface. The elongate gill-breathing larvae hunt among the leaf litter on the bottom of ponds. To pupate they surface and spin cocoons near the bank. Adults are good fliers and are sometimes attracted to lights.

RIPPLE RADAR

Despite having four eyes, two looking up and two looking down, whirligigs cannot actually see the water surface on which they swim. To enable them to locate struggling insect prey, their antennae sit flat on the surface and are equipped with an organ which reads the fine information in ripples, much like a radar. They can also pick up special mating-call ripples sent out by prospective mates.

Pond Skaters

Skaters need only the surface tension to support them on the water. This one is standing on a lily pad.

The most graceful of the surface-dwelling insects are the pond skaters, also known as water striders. They hold their short front and long back legs stiff, using them mainly to hold their elongate bodies up off the surface. A very long middle pair of legs serve as oars to row them along, not quite breaking the surface. Small movements of the back legs work like rudders for steering. The water-repelling hairs that cover most of the body help them not to break through the water tension.

OUT TO SEA

The waters of the open ocean would seem to be the worst of all places for an insect. However, one small group of water striders has adapted to this life. A few species never see land and spend their lives rowing on the surface of the Pacific Ocean. To escape fish they can make 12 cm high jumps off the surface. Related, but less adventurous, species live among mangroves and other coastal areas of Australia.

Behaviour and Mating

Skaters often live in groups. They tend to stay in the current of moving streams, maintaining their position on the flowing surface with apparently effortless rowing. Sooner or later insects that fall on the water float past and are caught alive or dead by the grasping front legs of the skaters. Being true bugs (see page 60), they use their sucking mouthparts to pierce the prey and suck out the liquid contents.

At mating time skaters drum the water surface, creating ripple 'messages' to be 'read' by the sensitive feet of prospective mates.

Young skaters are small copies of the adults and skate from birth. To escape danger, all skaters can make rapid prancing jumps across the surface.

SOCIAL INSECTS

What Is a Social Insect?

Social insect colonies are like a 'super-organism' acting as one, as demonstrated by the swarming behaviour of bees moving to a new nest.

Social insects are species that live in colonies with one or only a few females able to produce young. All other colony members are sterile. Their shape and size determines their 'caste' or group, such as workers and soldiers. They do all the nest building, hunting and caring for the young. The level of social organisation in the colony is so highly developed, it operates like a single 'superorganism'.

Subsocial Insects

The extreme organisation of social insects has evolved from simpler behaviour known as subsocial. For example some bugs, earwigs and beetles defend their eggs and young but the cycle is repeated anew with each generation rather than leading to an ongoing defended colony. Many wasps and subsocial bees group their separate nests together but do not give up their individual ability to reproduce.

In response to chemical signals, an entire ant colony moves larvae to higher ground.

Social Insects

At the pinnacle of social evolution are the termites, ants and honeybees. They build complex nests for the long-term survival of the colony and produce offspring biologically suited to different types of work. Among termites and some ants the reproductive 'queen' can be the sole parent of a colony for decades.

How Do Social Insects Communicate?

Social insects mostly communicate by exuding chemical smells called pheromones. Each carries a different message. Every need, from finding the way home to seeking food or help in battle, is chemically conveyed.

Chemical signals vary in complexity from a few common messages shared by subsocial wasps to the rich 'vocabulary' of ant colonies.

Each caste has its own smell and the pungency in the colony gives an indication of the relative numbers of each caste. In a termite colony, for example, the smell of the soldier caste may become weak following lost battles; the number of eggs developing into soldiers then automatically increases. Similarly new queen bees are produced from normal eggs that are fed the right chemical mix in the so-called 'royal jelly' (see page 33). Queens exude a chemical smell that defines the colony. All members of the colony carry this smell with them.

The Ant Perfumery

Ants always exchange messages about food and danger when meeting on their scent-marked trails.

Ants have the most complex language. They produce pheromones in glands all over their body. As foraging workers and soldiers leave the nest they lay an odour trail to return by. If they find food, a new layer of 'food-this-way' odour is overlaid on the way back. Passing ants are given a taste of the food so they can trace the new trail.

A new nest site heralds a 'recruiting trail' odour. Sometimes the scent-maker literally picks up and carries other ants back to the job.

The strongest scents are for emergencies. These intensify with proximity to the danger. The formic acid smell of many ants is one of these.

Why Do Bees Dance?

Bees 'dance' to communicate with each other. A bee returning to the hive will tell others in the nest about good sources of pollen. It performs one of several different dances on the vertical honeycomb, while other bees gather around and stroke it with their antennae.

A simple circular dance tells of flowers close by. No direction is given but the pollen scent on her may be enough indication of where to go. To describe distant sources, the bee does a figure-of-eight motion. At the top of the figure is the position of the sun as seen from the nest entrance, and the direction of the vertical line down the middle is the angle away from the sun. Because this dance is performed in the near dark of the hive, the vibration of the waggling bee and pheromone messages also help convey the picture.

In the depths of the hive, a bee tells of good flowers.

Ants

Best known of the Australian ants, the fiercely biting bull ant. Inset: Prime cut: tough meat ants dismember a cane toad.

Ants are essentially wasps with a complex social structure that includes a wingless caste known as a worker. They nest in colonies, mainly underground but also in logs, crevices and joined-leaf nests. There may be thousands of ants in a colony, each with one queen attended by workers in her chamber, where she lays eggs continuously. Workers are sterile females that care for the eggs and grub-like larvae in brood chambers or forage outside with larger workers known as soldiers.

Adult ants eat only liquid food, mainly nectar, honeydew or the blood of insect prey. They have a second large 'social' stomach which accommodates liquid food for workers in the nest. The solid food, like insects or seeds, is brought back whole or dismembered and fed to the larvae.

LOCKJAW

The bizarre snap-jaw ants have long straight mandibles that they can lock wide open. To strike at prey or foe the ant releases the lock and the jaws snap shut audibly in 0.002 of a second, mushing up their prey's insides.

Annual Mating and Home-making

Once a year all the local colonies of a species make two winged castes: fertile young queens and short-lived males. The colonies synchronise huge nuptial flights to disperse the species. After mating, males die. Females build new nests and start colonies. The first generation is vulnerable to starvation and predators. The queen nurtures them through to adult workers, who then look after her and take over nest building.

Termites

These termites, notorious for munching through wooden houses, are often wrongly called white ants. Inset: The home of harmless grass-eating termites.

Termites are the greatest architects of the insect world. In the northern grasslands they build mounds up to 6 m tall. Most of the mound is composed of hollow chimneys which regulate the internal temperature and humidity levels, a bit like our air-conditioning. The main chambers are at or below ground level and can house millions of termites. The so-called 'magnetic' termites build vertical flat rectangular nests that align north–south so perfectly that the morning and evening sun warms them but the hot midday sun hits only the thin edge. Many of Australia's 350 termite species live in wood or small underground chambers.

Life in the Colony

A termite colony consists of a queen, grossly distended into a huge egg-laying machine able to produce thousands of eggs a day, and her 'king', with up to millions of sterile workers and soldiers. Members of the colony feed mainly on wood or grass and sometimes on fungus grown in special nest gardens.

Sunlight kills termites, so most are nocturnal. They usually build enclosed mud tunnels from the nest to their food for added climate and predator control. To make new nests colonies produce a fertile winged caste which leaves the colony on a synchronised mating flight that usually occurs once a year.

LONG LIVE THE QUEEN

Termite colonies can survive a long time. One mound in the Northern Territory is known to be over 100 years old. The oldest recorded Australian queen, fed and groomed by her workers, lived 17 years. In this time she may have laid over 20 million eggs.

How Do Termites Defend Themselves?

Spinifex Termite workers repair a damaged nest, while 'glue'-spraying soldiers guard the breach outside.

Termites are soft, blind and slow. Every insect-eating animal loves to eat them. Some, especially ants, are always nearby waiting to take advantage of any weakness, so nests must be tough. Only a few specialist hunters, like echidnas, are strong enough to dig into them.

To forage outside the nest termites build covered tunnel-like walkways or stay out of sight inside the food source, such as a tree branch. When such precautions fail, the soldier caste defends the nest and food-gathering workers.

Termite Tactics

Even though some termite soldiers have large, hard heads with strong, sometimes twisted mandibles, in wars with ants termites' soft bodies make them easy targets. One defensive strategy is to sacrifice huge numbers in battle: wave upon wave of soldiers keep the enemy at bay, while workers repair the breach in the nest.

In Asia there are termite species with no soldiers. Their workers literally explode when cornered in battle, covering enemies with their slimy innards. However, the best defence systems belong to the so-called 'nasute' termites – for example, Spinifex Termites – which have strange pointy heads with no visible jaws. Most of the head is occupied by a gland which produces a sticky, and probably poisonous, glue-like liquid. The termites spray this liquid out through a turret-like snout. Attacking ants get tangled and irritated and slow down. This can turn the tide of the attack.

A Spinifex Termite soldier shows its 'glue pump' head, used to spray enemies with sticky fluids.

HONEY GUIDES

Unless pollinated by wind, flowers must attract insects to do the job. They may do this with a gift of sugars, a strong scent and/or showy petals. Insects see colours differently from us – shifted more towards the ultraviolet end of the spectrum. While red flowers appear black and uninteresting to a bee, some 'dull' flowers positively glow. Under ultraviolet light, lines that guide bees directly to pollen are visible on many flowers: these are 'honey guides'.

Do Cuckoo Wasps Act Like Cuckoos?

Yes. Like their bird namesakes, most of the 80 Australian species of these beautiful, little-known wasps lay their eggs in other species' nests, especially those of mud wasps. The cuckoo wasp larvae hatch early and eat the host larvae before they can pupate. If two cuckoo wasp females lay their eggs in the one nest, the hatchlings fight to the death.

Cuckoo wasps have bright metallic bodies, often shimmering green-blue. Because they can roll themselves into a smooth ball that even big wasps cannot grasp, they mostly walk brazenly into inhabited nests. Others dig into sealed nests.

Defence posture of the cuckoo wasp: rolled up, it presents a slippery armour-plating.

Do Social Insects Tolerate Trespassers?

The well-provisioned and safe nests of social insects are tempting places for many free-loader guest insects to live. Hundreds of species of beetles, some wasps, flies and others live in ant and termite nests, with a few sharing bees' nests.

Insect Hospitality

Guests of ants often mimic ant smells so as not to be rejected. Some guests exude nourishing, addictive fluids from special hairs to pacify their hosts. In times of danger addicted ant workers may save their guests before their own larvae.

The various insects that are guests of termites, called termitophiles, use similar ploys, and some even mimic the termite shape. Termite workers feed them and their larvae in return for the addictive fluids, which are also a source of food.

Not all guests behave well. Some specialist beetles with tough, slippery bodies that ants cannot grasp or damage, simply steal food or even the hosts' larvae.

SOCIAL BEETLES

On the evolutionary path towards fully social insects there are many subsocial groups where individuals cooperate but do not organise into societies with a queen and sterile workers. For example, several families of passilid beetle live together in a rotten log. There they care for their young and all adults share the tasks of food gathering, tunnelling and defence.

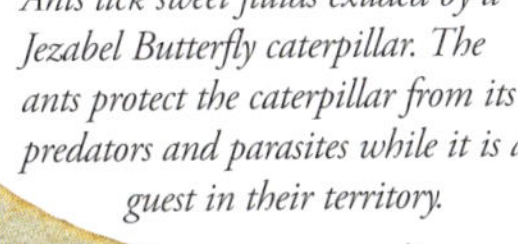

Ants lick sweet fluids exuded by a Jezabel Butterfly caterpillar. The ants protect the caterpillar from its predators and parasites while it is a guest in their territory.

Paper Wasps

Paper wasps keep to themselves unless the nest is disturbed. Inset: A small paper wasp nest under a leaf shows the larvae, heads up, in their brood cells.

Paper wasps are a group of 34 Australian species within a family of hunting wasps with varying degrees of social behaviour. Most are about 1 cm long with striking combinations of yellow and black patterns.

Paper Nests

They build communal nests out of 'card', a strong paper-like substance made of pulped plant fibre and saliva. The nests are under leaves, in rock overhangs, underground, and a favourite place for some species is under the eaves of houses. They range from a simple disk of paper cells to many, even spiral, layers. Some are enclosed 'cities' of layers housing thousands of individuals.

Social Organisation

Paper wasps are known as eusocial: they do not have complex multicaste societies like ants and termites. The females in a typical nest all look the same but the strongest female exudes pheromones that suppress the breeding potential of the others. She becomes the only egg layer or queen. The worker wasps defend the nest with stings. They search for caterpillars to feed the larvae but eat only nectar themselves. The larvae 'ask' for food by exuding a liquid that the workers, and especially the queen, need and are rewarded with pre-masticated caterpillars.

In cold regions nests die back in winter, leaving a solitary queen to restart the nest in spring but much of Australia is warm enough for year-round activity.

Honeybees

A honeybee collecting pollen on its back legs. Inset: A honeybee collecting sugars by licking scale insects, which exude honeydew.

The European Honeybee was introduced to Australia in the early days of European settlement. It has characteristic yellow and black stripes, and a barbed stinger which, when used, detaches and disembowels the bee, killing it.

Honeybees have evolved the most complex organisation of all social bees. Workers use resins and wax to construct nests with a vertical honeycomb of storage and brood cells. A typical nest may house 50 000 all-female workers, a few developing males (drones) and one queen. The queen lays up to 1500 eggs a day and produces pheromones to keep workers sterile and prevent development of new queens. The workers live for six weeks, undertaking a series of age-related tasks. Newly hatched workers only clean the nest but soon take up nursing and nest building. In two weeks they become nest guards and receive pollen from foraging bees. From middle age, they forage themselves.

The Fight To Be Queen

When a queen weakens, pheromone levels drop to allow development of new queen cells. Rich 'royal jelly' is a chemically complex food made by workers and fed to all larvae for a few days but only the larvae in queen cells get it all their lives. This causes them to develop into the larger, fertile queens. When these **hatch** the reigning queen is forced to leave the nest to face an uncertain future.

Newly **hatched** queens fight each other to the death. A spectacular mating flight follows: within a flying, writhing ball of bee bodies, the victorious queen mates with several drones to store a good genetic mix of sperm to last her an egg-laying life of up to five years. The drones die after mating.

How Do Native Bees Live?

Australia has over 1600 species of bees, all of which are native except for the introduced European Honeybee. All bees are pollinators, and most, unlike the European Honeybee, are solitary. They build simple single-celled or branched-celled nests in plant stems, tree holes or underground. They provision the cells with nectar, lay one egg in each, and seal them up, usually dying before the progeny emerges.

Some burrowing bees live in communal burrows but not in a social order. Leaf-cutter bees neatly cut up colourful leaves, including rose petals, for nest building. Carpenter bees include some very large, metallic-coloured bees reminiscent of bumblebees.

The 6 mm long sugarbag bees are among the few native honey-makers.

One of the solitary native bees collects nectar for its larvae.

Native Honeybees

The only native bees that form large, complex societies belong to the same family as European Honeybees. Native honeybees are small, black species known as 'stingless' bees or 'sugarbag' bees. They make nests in logs and other chambers, with separate honey storage and brood areas, and can number over 10 000. They do not sting and their honey, less sweet and more runny, is now commercially available.

Can Wasps Cause Paralysis?

Many hunting wasps are adept at causing paralysis, but only to creatures their own size. Some wasps which parasitise free-living insects, like caterpillars, may only lay their eggs on them and then fly away. Specialist hunters, like the spider wasps and mud wasps, sting their prey. The poison causes paralysis but not death, and the hapless prey becomes a living food source for the carnivorous wasp larvae, sealed up in mud pots or underground nests.

What Is a 'Velvet' Ant?

If you come across a lone large 'ant' with bright, often metallic colours – beware. Chances are it is not an ant but a wingless female of a wasp family known as velvet ants. The bold colours advertise one of the more painful stings of the insect world.

Wingless females search for the pupae of various insects, especially other wasps, to parasitise. Protected by their tough exoskeleton they enter the burrows of sand wasps and the nests of mud wasps. The larger winged males seek females on the wing. Mating involves a flight with the female being carried by the male.

The female velvet ant walks jerkily as she looks for other wasp nests to invade.

A green tree ant–mimicking spider (left) picks off straggling ants.

When Is an Ant a Spider?

Ants are a poor choice of prey. They are fierce insects that run in large groups and are armed with stings and other chemical deterrents. Many insects protect themselves by mimicking ants, but spiders, too, pretend to be ants. Species of several families, especially the jumping spiders, have constricted ant-like waists and copy the telltale twitchy running gait of ants. Spiders often disguise their extra pair of legs – spiders have four pairs, insects only three – by carrying their front legs up like fake antennae. Running with ants protects spiders from their normal predators. There is also another advantage: it's easier to catch and eat ants when you're pretending to be one. Some ant-mimicking spiders even specialise in ant prey.

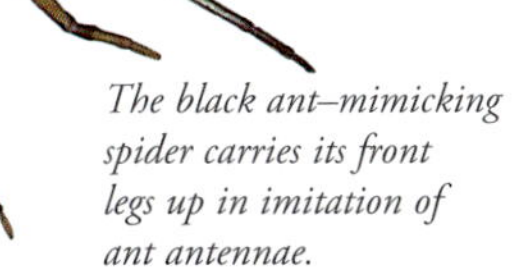

The black ant–mimicking spider carries its front legs up in imitation of ant antennae.

WEIGHTLIFTING

Ants can lift 50 times their own weight. The lifting ability of insects is due to their brilliant body structure – muscles attached on the inside of a strongly jointed armour. This works a bit like a crane. Holding the insect weightlifting record is a species of elephant beetle, which can lift over 800 times its own weight!

What Do Mud Wasps Do?

Two families of wasps have evolved the habit of constructing nests built from mud. The mud daubers are known for making elongate mud chambers, often between two surfaces to save on building time. Inside are separate chambers provisioned with paralysed spiders to feed to the wasp larvae. Females build the nests alone, although the males of some species stand guard while she hunts.

A mud-dauber wasp gathers wet mud to build its nest. Other species may carry water and soil separately.

Potter Wasps

The majority of mud wasps belong to a group known as potter wasps, whose nests are often built under rock overhangs or in the corners of houses. These can be quite large; 'pots' 10 cm or more are not uncommon and the wasps often reuse them seasonally. For each larva the adult builds a new, often trumpet-shaped entrance. Having deposited a paralysed caterpillar and egg within, the wasp seals it off. While we might appreciate wasps hunting caterpillars in our gardens, some mud wasps have the annoying habit of nesting among tools, on bicycles, in furniture and, more recently, in computers.

When Did Bees and Wasps Evolve?

Although some insect forms have been around for 400 million years, today's showy and abundant insects, like butterflies, wasps and flies, did not evolve until the evolution of flowering plants around 130 million years ago. A complex relationship arose between flowering plants and insects. The plants, laden with nectar, gave the insects their energy-rich food in exchange for help with spreading their pollen. This enabled the insects to rapidly diversify along with the flowers. Prior to this the main plants were the often tough and/or poisonous cycads and ferns – not a good diet for insects. Bees, the pollinating specialists, are currently the most modern insects, although they've already been on the planet for over 35 million years.

Often found on ceilings, the 'pots' of mud daubers, each imprisoning a paralysed spider.

Do All Wasps Sting?

The vast majority of Australia's 12 000 odd species of wasps cannot sting humans and go about their work largely unnoticed. Most of them are performing beneficial tasks by parasitising other, sometimes pesky or injurious insects, and by pollinating native and crop plants.

The main stingers are the social species whose sterile females defend their nests with a modified ovipositor, a stiletto-like organ that would otherwise be used for egg laying. Paper wasps, the European Honeybee and ants, which are essentially wingless wasps, are the main culprits. While bees have a barbed stinger which after a single use wrenches out the bee's guts, killing it, the paper wasps and ants have pointy ones which are reusable.

A giant potter wasp builds a funnel-shaped entrance for each chamber.

Why Are People Scared of Wasps?

The European Wasp may sting if disturbed while eating our food.

Wasps have a reputation for causing painful stings and some may even be deadly. However, bee, wasp and ant stings are generally not dangerous. For most people they result only in temporary pain, swelling and itching.

In rare cases the venom causes an allergic reaction, which can be life threatening. The first sting may sensitise the immune system so it overreacts on the next occasion. It's particularly nasty when a wasp gets into a soft drink container in search of sugar. If the wasp is swallowed, it may sting the tongue or throat. An allergic reaction could cause enough swelling to restrict breathing. The worst offender is the introduced European Wasp, whose range is slowly spreading from south-eastern Tasmania and the Perth area. Our own paper wasps are less dangerous but have the memorable habit of defending the nest as a swarm.

NEVERENDING WASP STORY

In Europe the fiercely stinging European Wasps make little paper nests in ground crevices and, except for the hibernating queen, die off every winter. However, in our warm climate the nests grow continuously and swell from the typical few hundred to hundreds of thousands of individuals, in nests metres long.

The Hunters

Who Are the Hunters?

Like lions, ground beetles run down their prey and tear it up with their strong mandibles.

Since insects are so famous for their sometimes destructive plant-eating habits, it is surprising to learn that there are actually more insect groups that hunt for a living than eat plants. Praying mantids, dragonflies and assassin bugs are carnivorous at all their life stages.

Aquatic insects are often hunters during all life stages. Names like 'water scorpion' and 'fish-killer bugs' speak for themselves but even the delicately named ladybird beetles are actually major killers of aphids. Many families of beetles, wasps, flies, crickets and the majority of ants are hunters. Even among insect groups well known for their plant-feeding habits, there are carnivorous exceptions. For example, some moths have killer caterpillars. Indeed, quite a few insects are carnivorous as larvae and plant-eaters when adults.

How Do Insects Hunt?

Running after prey in the style of the big cats, as ground beetles do (above), is uncommon insect behaviour. While dragonflies and hunting flies seize their food on the wing, more often insects wait for their prey to come to them. Praying mantids wait with great patience, often disguised as part of the foliage. Assassin bugs, fish-killer bugs and the delicate mantis flies also wait patiently for their prey; all have similar spiny raptorial forelegs to mantids. Hunting beetles, like ladybirds, simply walk among herds of docile aphid prey.

Some insects use traps: ant lions, for example, build slippery conical sandpits and the aquatic larvae of caddisflies spin silk nets. When all else fails, some sneaky hunters resort to stealing prey from other insect predators. Ants are the biggest robbers, often going on raiding parties to steal prey from another species. Some flies and dragonflies do it in flight.

The spiny front legs of praying mantids have a snap-jaw action that impales prey on the first strike.

Suck or Chew?

Not all carnivorous insects use chewing mandibles. Hunting bugs, like assassin bugs, have a modified beak-like tube called a rostrum through which they inject digestive enzymes, and sometimes poison, to kill and mush up their prey before sucking it up.

Who Are the Main Predators of Insects?

This greenish mushy lump is all that is left of a cricket caught at night by a huntsman spider.

The extremely rapid breeding rate of insects would soon have us wading knee deep in them if not for the complex web of predators that feed on them. Many birds, lizards, mammals and even fish hunt insects. Bats, marsupial mice, swallows, echidnas and numbats are Australia's most specialised insect-eaters.

However, these large animals would not make much of a dent if not for the predation and parasitism within the invertebrate world. A large percentage of insects do not develop to adulthood because insect parasites kill their eggs and larvae. Hunting insects like praying mantids, flies and ground beetles also eat other insects. Spiders are the chief invertebrate hunters of insects.

Co-evolution of insects and their prey has resulted in some amazing adaptations: some moths emit interference sounds to confuse bat echolocation, while many insects, like stink bugs, carry stores of protective poisons.

BEETLE BOMBS

Bombardier beetles have the most elaborate and improbable defence of all insects. Several body chambers store chemicals which, when mixed with an enzyme, literally explode. A turret-like cannon at its rear can direct this hot, audible and foul-smelling puff of smoke in any direction, repelling other insects and even frogs.

Do Insects Use Light to Attract Prey?

A glow worm surrounded by strands of its home-made web covered with sticky drops.

Fireflies emit light only to attract mates rather than prey; it's like a visible bird song.

However, the larvae of a group of fungus gnats – small, midge-like flies – glow to hunt. These larvae are called glow worms. They live in overhangs and caves, which they drape with strands or loose webs of silk covered in sticky drops. Insects flying towards their glowing bodies are trapped and eaten. There are species of this gnat in Australia but the famous Waitomo flies of New Zealand caves are the strongest light emitters in this group.

Praying Mantids

Mantids can easily catch prey bigger than themselves, like this dragonfly. Inset: The poised raptorial front legs of Australia's largest mantid.

Praying mantids are the best known predators of the insect world. The 160 or so species come in many shapes, from flat, green leaf-like ones to brown, skinny stick-like ones. All are well adapted for hunting. Most have large eyes with almost 360-degree vision. Their front legs are equipped with two sets of spines that face into each other when the legs are in the 'praying' folded position. Legs adapted for grabbing like this are called raptorial, from the raptors, or hunting birds, like eagles.

Hunting and Life Cycle

Most mantids blend in well with a variety of vegetation. They wait motionless, observing potential prey, waiting for it to come to them, or making very slow, delicate movements towards it. When close enough their front legs spring out fast enough to catch even nervous prey like flies, impaling them in a death grip.

Females extrude foam with their eggs. They weave the foam into an ootheca – a bag-shaped case half their own size. The foam sticks to a branch and sets hard, protecting the 10 to 400 eggs from predators. While the adults are usually winged, the nymphs are squatter, smaller and wingless. In their most vulnerable early stages they sometimes mimic ants. Running along the ground or on tree trunks, protected by this ruse, they are happy to get closer to ants, all the better to eat them.

INSECT CHAMELEONS

Many mantids blend in with the bark of their tree homes. However, after a bushfire, when insects in a blackened, burnt-out area can stand out dangerously, some mantids change colour over a period of days to match their new dark backgrounds. They are among the first insects to return and ambush the other more visible insects.

Ant Lions

Ant lions are the larvae (above) of long, winged insects (top right). They build conical pits in dry sand (bottom right) to catch ants.

Ant lion is the name given to the larvae of certain long, thin, winged insects. The perfect conical sandpits of ant lions are common all over Australia. They hide in the sand at the bottom of the pit. Ant lions are flat and sand coloured and have a small head with huge, tusk-like jaws. Sandpits need to be in dry loose sand, so more species are found in deserts. However, any sandy rock overhang or artificial shelter, like under the house, will have telltale pits. As an ant walks by, the loose sand on the rim of the pit gives way and it slides in. From below the ant lion flicks more sand at the struggling ant until it falls down into the ant lion's waiting jaws. These grooved mandibles inject digesting enzymes and the ant lion sucks up the contents before flinging out the dry, shrivelled body.

Life Cycle

Ant lions live from one to several years, with only three larval stages before pupating in a cocoon in the sand. The adults are elongate, delicate insects with long, membranous wings reminiscent of dragonflies. Depending on the species, adults range from 10 to 50 mm long. Unlike dragonflies, they fold their wings along their body when at rest. Adults are active at night but little is known of their habits. They are probably predatory. The sexes find each other by pheromone scent and some species inexplicably produce another scent similar to ants.

Do Scorpion-flies Sting?

Despite their name, scorpion-flies don't sting. Their name is derived from appearance only. Some males do have a fearsome-looking, bulbous scorpion-like 'tail' but this is actually an elaborate set of genitalia. None are known to use the tail to attack.

In Australia many species are called 'hanging flies' because they hang vertically by their front legs, while their modified back legs dangle ready to strike at passing insects. The rear feet, or tarsi, have a curved hook that closes onto a toothed surface, similar to the grasping front legs of praying mantids. Mouthparts are elongated into a beak-like rostrum which both chews and sucks.

The larvae look like caterpillars and live on the ground among litter or in burrows, feeding mainly on decaying plants and dead insects. An odd wingless species in Tasmania lives above the snowline feeding on mosses.

Scorpion-flies spend much time hanging from their front legs, ready to strike at insects flying by with their modified, spiny back 'feet'.

Why Are Lacewings Good for Your Garden?

Lacewings are delicate flying insects with large, finely veined clear wings. As adults, many only feed on nectar but as larvae most are predators of other insects. Typical hunting larvae are elongate with long pointy mandibles modified into tubes through which they suck prey dry. Some have the grizzly habit of disguising their body with a covering of dry husks from their victims.

Soft insects like aphids are their favourite food, so having them in your garden is always beneficial. Adults of the related mantis flies are also helpful. They have the same raptorial front legs as praying mantids and often beautifully patterned bodies and eyes.

The commonest adult lacewings are the bright 'golden eyes', most of which are predators.

Larvae suck aphids dry and 'wear' their shrivelled bodies as disguise.

When Is an Insect a Mushroom?

A paper wasp killed by fungus sprouting from it.

Various insects, from cockroaches to beetles, eat fungi. But some fungi also prey on insects. Up to 70 per cent of insects have some part of their life cycle in or near the soil. During this phase fungi may enter insect larvae by slowly forcing their way between the separate armour segments of the exoskeleton. This often happens after a moult, when the larvae are all soft and squishy. The fungi slowly eat the larvae from the inside, then send out a white cloud of spores from the dead bodies.

Other more unusual fungi hunt flying insects like flies and wasps. Their airborne spores penetrate the tough exoskeleton and grow inside. To reproduce, the fungi somehow encourage the weakened insect to climb to the end of a branch, where it dies, seemingly in mid-stride. Little mushrooms then burst through the exoskeleton and spray their spores into the air to be dispersed by the wind and to land on other insects.

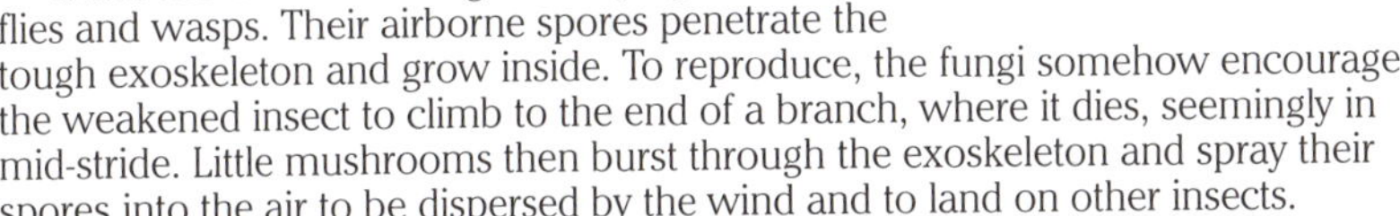

Some fungi are such effective killers that they have been developed into a form of bio-insecticide. Aphids in Europe, cotton pests in America and plague locusts in Australia are commonly sprayed with a fungi and oil mixture to keep infestations down.

Do Female Mantids Really Eat Their Mates?

This is one of the great urban myths – or is it? Like many fabulous stories, it has some basis. The majority of male mantids survive mating but it is advantageous to the female to eat the odd one as this provides a large amount of protein for the development of her eggs. It has also been shown that when she eats the head – always the first part to go – the rest of the body reverts to the control of individual 'sub-brains' in the body, and the male actually continues to mate more vigorously.

Needless to say, it's to the male's advantage to live to see another day and mate with other females. So males approach females with caution, jumping onto them away from their raptorial forelegs, and jumping off quickly afterwards.

In a seemingly ominous but unrelated twist, females of a few mantid species can reproduce without males. In such cases they always produce only female offspring. They simply lay unfertilised eggs that always hatch into females.

NUPTIAL GIFTS

Male scorpion-flies use pheromones to attract a female but she chooses a mate based on the quality of his gifts. These are usually juicy insects. The females of some species apparently never catch their own prey. The pressure to provide nuptial gifts leads some males to steal from each other, and to the unchivalrous act of holding onto the prey in order to retain some leftovers for another female.

Tiger Beetles

Tiger beetles have large, snapping jaws. Inset: Most tiger beetles hunt by day, but this mating pair of stout tigers from the interior hunt at night.

This is one of the more apt names in the insect world. These long-legged, huge-jawed beetles run down insect prey on the open ground, using their large eyes to spot movement in their territories. Some species prefer the beach. Their long legs keep them up off the hot sand, while the heat helps power their nervous bursts of activity. Other species run up and down tree trunks, and a few are nocturnal ground hunters in the arid interior of Australia.

Vicious Larvae

The larvae, which live in vertical burrows, also terrorise other insects. They have very large, heavily armoured heads which usually sit flush with the ground. Their eyes have 360-degree vision. When a hapless insect walks by, the tiger beetle larva jumps out backwards like a jack-in-the-box, grabs it with long, curved jaws and retreats back to a deeper part of the burrow. Sometimes larvae are lazy: they just sit lower down in the burrow and wait for prey to fall in.

To prevent predators dragging it out into the open in a struggle, the larva anchors itself firmly to the burrow wall with a large hook in the middle of its back.

THE FASTEST RUNNER

Tiger beetles can run down a fly on a hot day. They are the fastest runners in the insect world. The record is held by an Australian tiger beetle that clocked at 2.5 m per second – about 9 km per hour. This works out to be 171 body lengths per second and is the equivalent of a 2 m-tall human running at 342 m per second, which equates with the speed of sound!

Ladybird Beetles

Only the cast skins of aphids remain on this flower patrolled by ladybirds. Inset: This ladybird is wallowing in its food, citrus mealybugs.

There are about 300 species of ladybirds in Australia. Most are hunters and have a reputation as beneficial insects as they especially enjoy eating soft insects like aphids, scale insects and mealybugs, many of which are pests of gardens and crops.

Life Cycle and Defence

Ladybirds lay their eggs on branches housing the best prey. As soon as larvae hatch they start eating the same diet as the adults. With seemingly limitless appetites, they devour large numbers of prey and pupate in only a few weeks. Some prey, like aphids, produce honeydew, which ants like so much they farm and protect the aphids and often attack the ladybirds. Well protected by their hard-domed, slippery bodies, ladybirds also use a rare chemical defence: sticky and apparently toxic blood exuded mainly from their 'knees', where they are most vulnerable to being grabbed by ants.

LADYBIRD WARRIORS

Late in the nineteenth century an Australian pest, the Cottony Cushion Scale Insect, was accidentally transported to California, where it threatened a huge citrus industry. An Australian scale insect-eating ladybird was sent to eradicate it in what was the first ever major biological control. It won the battle and other species of ladybirds have since been sent to America with similar successes.

How Many Spots?

Many ladybird common names are based on the number of spots they have. The Twenty-eight–spotted Ladybird is the current record holder. It also belongs to a rogue genus whose species eat plants and are pests of some of our favourite crops like potatoes and tomatoes.

Are Crickets Grasshoppers?

No. Crickets and grasshoppers belong to the same insect group and share many features. Both have toughened leathery forewings over flying membranous hindwings. Both, too, have large back legs often used for jumping, and strong chewing mouthparts.

Crickets, however, are nocturnal, and live anywhere from below ground to high in trees. They eat any plant matter from leaves to seeds; some even hunt. Grasshoppers are active during the day (diurnal). They eat almost entirely grass and low vegetation among which they live.

Crickets have antennae that are over 30 segments long, compared to the very short ones on grasshoppers. Female crickets also have an ovipositor, a sword-like appendage for laying eggs in plants and crevices, whereas grasshoppers use four small triangular plates at the rear to dig holes for eggs in the soil. Crickets' night songs can be complex and melodious but most grasshoppers need to hide from predators during the day and so they limit their songs to short clicks and chirps.

The bush cricket's long antennae signify it's not a grasshopper. .

Who Are the King Crickets?

Most crickets and katydids are plant eaters but some hunt other insects. Among these are the king crickets, a small family of about 15 species. King crickets use their forelegs to grasp and their large jaws to subdue prey. Most are large, some are wingless and all have enlarged heads and mandibles. The mandibles of some males are as long as the head. While all crickets have spines along the back legs, used to kick back at attackers, king crickets have extra inward-pointing spines on the forelegs to impale and hold prey. They are nocturnal, and best left alone as their bite is ferocious.

King crickets can overpower prey as big as themselves, so a cockroach is an easy meal.

KNEES WITH EARS

Crickets and grasshoppers have their 'ears' in odd places. Grasshoppers have tympanal organs – drum-like skins on their exoskeleton beneath their forewings. Cricket 'ears' are exposed on their forelegs – look for the slit just under their 'knees'.

Who Are the Most Aggressive Ants?

Even one of the largest praying mantids is not able to defend itself against the organised attack of green tree ants.

The mention of exotic ants, with names like army ants, fire ants and the inexorable African driver ants, strikes fear into the hearts of humans. In Australia we tend to fear the sting of bull ants above all. But for sheer pugnacious will, the defensive bull ants fade into insignificance next to the little green tree ants of the tropics.

Battle Strategies

Luckily individual bites of green tree ants are not very painful compared to those of bull ants but hundreds could fall on you from the branches where they live as you brush past. Walk past their leaf nests and swarms run out to the edge and gesticulate madly with open jaws, ready for a fight. They instantly attack intruders of any size, even ants of the same species from other colonies. This creates 'no ant' zones around the territorial boundaries, with the outermost nests guarded by the oldest, most battle-expendable workers. The secret to their success is their cooperative battle strategy of spread-eagling intruders. Using their jaws, they grip and pin down all appendages, rendering even bull ants helpless. They then dismember the victim to feed to their babies.

Weavers

Green ants are also known as weaver ants because they literally weave their nests together using silk squeezed from their larvae. Some workers hold leaves together under tension while others walk about with larvae in their jaws, squeezing out silk in a zig-zag pattern to bind the leaves tight. A single colony may occupy 10 or more trees, dotted with small nests, all controlled by one queen.

Chains of perfectly cooperating green tree ants stretch and weave leaves together to build a nest.

LEMONADE ANTS

Although a green tree ant might bite you, you can bite back. The bodies of green tree ants contain ascorbic acid (vitamin C), which tastes very agreeably like sherbet. Aboriginal people use them as both food and medicine. They squeeze whole nests underwater to make a citrusy drink or simply bite off the tangy bum.

Assassin Bugs

An assassin bug slowly prowls its territory. Inset: The powerful beak, or rostrum, is used to impale and suck out prey.

These deadly assassins are appropriately named. They are the only family of terrestrial bugs to be completely predatory. They have an elongate body flattened from above with a small, but protruding head. Like all true bugs (see page 60) their mouthparts form a beak-like structure called a rostrum, which is extra large in assassins. Having pounced on prey with their front legs, assassins impale it on their rostrum before pumping it full of digestive saliva and sucking out the contents. Assassins hatch from eggs as nymphs which look and behave just like small adults.

Hunting

Most assassin bugs prowl stealthily along plants or on the ground in daytime, slowly creeping up on prey. Some use camouflage, secreting themselves in flowers or blending with bark. One overseas species is known to mimic scents which lure bees to their death. An Australian species exudes a fluid attractive to ants. Its soothing effect makes ants easy targets. Another species that looks a bit like mud from a termite mound and apparently even mimics the general scent of termites, adeptly picks the unsuspecting termites off at their entrance. Another group of thin and delicate assassins has evolved raptorial forelegs like those of praying mantids. One of these robs spider webs while others hunt mosquitoes.

A BLISTERING BITE

Although not aggressive insects, assassins will bite if handled. With each bite they inject fluids similar to our stomach acids. Designed to dissolve living tissue, this fluid is usually reserved for digesting prey. While the dose is minute, it is enough to cause memorable pain and a nasty blister.

Robber Flies

A female robber fly eats her male suitor to provide protein for the development of her eggs. Inset: Robber fly 'feet' are armed with sharp claws.

There are 650 species of these medium to large flies, which are renowned for their formidable hunting skills. Among them is the largest fly in Australia, with a wingspan of up to 80 mm.

Adult flies lurk on the tips of branches or leaves, watching for flying insects with their very large eyes. Unlike dragonflies, which mostly hunt on the wing, robber flies suddenly accelerate from a standing start to catch unwary insects flying by. Soaring up above the insect, they swoop, grabbing it with long, clawed legs, before delivering a fatal bite to the back of the neck. They inject a poison to kill and a digestive enzyme to liquefy the prey. They then suck it dry, either partly in flight or while perched, sometimes hanging nonchalantly by one leg. Beekeepers dislike robbers because some species have a fondness for bees. Flies and wasps are also a favourite prey. Not even other predators, including the larger dragonflies, are immune to their powerful attacks.

Little is known about the maggot-like larvae, which live mainly on the ground; some are predators and others are scavengers.

TOUGH AND DEVIOUS

Despite being adept and feared hunters, robber flies live in the open and so they remain vulnerable to big predators, like birds. Some species have evolved an excellent resemblance to wasps, which makes birds think twice before attacking. This ruse has the added advantage of making it easier for robbers to make a meal of unwary wasps.

Plant Feeders

Who Are the Plant Feeders?

About a third of all insects feed on plants directly. Moths, butterflies, beetles, grasshoppers and bugs are among the most numerous. Apart from the more obvious leaf feeders, like caterpillars and sap-sucking bugs, there are many immature stages of insects that feed inside living tree trunks and branches, as well as in and on roots.

Evolution

The earliest plants colonised the land just before the first insects left the sea, around 400 million years ago. Because there was limited plant variety and flowers evolved much later, more insect groups evolved habits other than plant feeding, such as hunting and scavenging. Plants and insects are in an ongoing evolutionary catch-up game. Plants continually evolve new ways to repel insects, such as by developing tough, waxy, hairy, spiny, sticky or poisonous leaves. Insects have always found ways to survive and even benefit from these defences. For example, many caterpillars store the leaf poisons to protect themselves from predators.

How Do Insects Eat Plants?

Some caterpillars stay in groups for protection, thereby defoliating plants rapidly.

Most plant-eating insects possess hard mandibles to chew leaves, or to tunnel into and eat wood. Many adult insects, such as butterflies and moths, feed solely on nectar, or not at all, but their larvae – the caterpillars – eat plants. Grasshoppers chew leaves from the outer edge. Some beetles eat out holes or complete layers of leaves, leaving dotty or skeletonised patterns. Bugs insert their tubular mouthparts into plants to drink the sugar-rich fluids within their cells. Some plants actually pump the fluids into insects like aphids and cicadas, who then ooze out the excess undigested juice, which other insects like ants love.

Rose aphids suck the sap from soft growing tips, and so weaken plants.

When Is a Grasshopper a Locust?

Of the 700 species of grasshoppers in Australia, about five carry the name locust. They look the same as grasshoppers but behave differently in two ways. Firstly, locusts are adapted to swiftly take advantage of fresh green growth by breeding up very fast. Secondly, when numbers build up to a certain threshold, the normally solitary nymphs become 'gregarious': they come together in 'bands' and methodically eat their way across the green landscape like a tide, destroying everything in their path. Adult locusts also stay together as they denude an area, sometimes migrating as a swarm to find more food.

Having fattened up on the local vegetation, female plague locusts lay eggs into the desert soil.

LONG JUMP
The most efficient animal motion, other than flying, is hopping. Grasshoppers' powerful jumping back legs have an incredible 97 per cent efficiency in transferring stored energy into motion, allowing them to jump about 30 times their own length, or an equivalent of about 60 m for a human.

There are destructive outbreaks of Australian Plague Locusts in the southern and eastern half of the continent every few years. Luckily the much larger Spur-throated Locust, related to the African locusts, plagues much less frequently.

How Far Can Locusts Migrate?

Numbers of the Australian Plague Locust normally build up when drought-breaking rains in the interior hatch overwintering eggs and provide green grass for the nymphs to eat. Often by the time locusts reach adulthood the grasses have dried up and they must migrate in search of food. Swarms of hundreds of millions can take advantage of low-pressure air systems creating winds to lift off as one, flying on these winds overnight for up to 500 km. In some years this can happen two or three times in one season, with further breeding multiplying the swarm by 10 times every generation. In the most spectacular migration recorded, in 1973, a swarm took off in New South Wales on winds which proved so strong that the locusts wound up swimming in the Bass Strait and even landing in Tasmania!

A single plague locust looks harmless but in large numbers they wreak havoc.

Grasshoppers

Pandanus Grasshoppers inhabit wetlands. Inset: Tropical monkey grasshoppers sit with their legs in this characteristically odd pose.

The majority of grasshoppers belong to one large family but six other families have related insects with names like 'monkey' and 'pygmy' grasshoppers. Most grasshoppers are long-winged insects with large jumping rear legs, though the thin monkey grasshoppers are all wingless.

Grasshoppers mainly eat grass but many species also eat shrubs, succulents and tree leaves. In dry country one group eats dead eucalyptus leaves. To camouflage themselves the nymphs even mimic the appearance of dead leaves.

Reproduction and Life Cycle

While not as loud or complex as the crickets, the short calls of male grasshoppers bring the sexes together. The female is larger than the male and has a set of four small, shovel-like plates at the tip of her abdomen. By extending the body at each segment join, she can use these plates to slowly dig a hole up to twice as deep as her length. She then lays 10 to 200 eggs encased in foam, which sets hard in the hole. Nymphs hatch after the weather warms or heavy rain has soaked the soil – the sign that there will be plenty of green grass to feed on. They grow through five moults before becoming adults.

WET PYGMIES

Most grasshoppers live on dry land, often in dry deserts. But about 70 species, known as pygmy grasshoppers, prefer a wetter environment. Most are under 10 mm long and feed on minute plants along the shores of streams and lakes. To escape predators, they can walk on water or even dive underwater.

Stick and Leaf Insects

Although stick and leaf insects typically have small wings, they do use them for flying and creating threatening displays. Inset: The Spiny Stick Insect is one of the fattest 'sticks' and is now sold worldwide as a pet.

Stick and leaf insects are among the best camouflage artists in nature. They mimic mainly sticks and bark but also grasses and leaves. Most of the 150 species are apparently uncommon as well as hard to spot, and many live in the canopy of trees. There are only a few species of leaf insects in Australia and they are so hard to find that most entomologists have never seen one.

All stick and leaf insects feed on green vegetation, usually at night, and keep still during the day. A few species change colour from light to dark depending on time of day, and a few gregarious species turn multicoloured when in big numbers.

Mating and Reproduction

Finding mates among such well-hidden creatures can be difficult. For some species of stick insect, no one has ever seen the male. Males of most species can fly, and in many cases females produce a pheromone that attracts them. But when all else fails, females lay unfertilised eggs which produce more females, identical clones of their mothers.

The randomly laid eggs have a remarkable resemblance to seeds, even those of the plants they sit on. Ants are fooled enough to help distribute the eggs along with their seed collections. Tiny nymphs uncoil from the egg, either the same season or up to three years later. They grow slowly through several moults, feeding on a wide range of plants, which makes them easy to keep as pets.

THE BIGGEST STICK

With thousands of tiny insects still awaiting discovery, it was a great surprise when Australia's longest insect was discovered only a few years ago. This monster stick insect from northern Queensland measures up to 60cm with outstretched legs, and lives a hidden life in the rainforest canopy.

So What Is a Bug?

Many people, especially Americans, refer to all insects as bugs. Bugs are, however, a distinct insect group characterised by mouthparts that form a tubular beak-like structure called a rostrum. They are divided into three main groups: the soft rounded aphids and scale insects; the harder elongate hoppers and cicadas; and the so-called true bugs, like stink bugs and shield bugs.

Harlequin Bugs have garish colours to warn predators of their nasty taste.

Where Do Cicadas Come From?

An adult cicada emerging from its nymph shell during a busy cicada season.

Australian summers are associated with what is sometimes a deafening cicada chorus. Children growing up on the east coast know about 'Green Grocers', 'Floury Bakers' or the coveted 'Black Prince'. These cicadas do not appear every year. Most of the 250 Australian species have cycles of several years, and remain hidden for the majority of that time.

Cicadas are sap-sucking bugs with beak-like mouthparts which can penetrate into the circulatory system of trees and suck the flowing sap. They absorb some sugars and release the rest of the fluid largely undigested. That's why it can feel like it's raining when you stand under a tree full of cicadas.

The often gregarious males call to the females using two large drum skin–like round plates called tympanums on the sides of their abdomens. A large, hollow cavity in the abdomen amplifies the sound. Females deposit eggs into slits on branches, and the brown hatchling nymphs fall to the ground and dig with huge, shovel-like front legs. They remain underground for several years feeding on the sap of tree roots and emerge on summer nights, leaving their telltale 'skins' on tree trunks and fences.

So Where's the Scale Insect?

Females of the Mango Scale hide under wax covers, while the elongate immature males are free living.

Have you ever noticed those little, waxy, sometimes coloured, flat spots and blobs on plants? These are the scales or shields under which 'scale' insects hide. This is a diverse group of bugs, that is, insects with sucking mouthparts. They have pale, soft, fat and sometimes almost featureless bodies, somewhat related to aphids. Females, and sometimes males, are wingless. They spend their lives hiding under the waxy scale created from the exuded excess sap they have sucked from plants. Many insects, but especially ants, often attend scale insects to feed on this excess.

Scale insects can seriously debilitate plants and transmit a variety of plant diseases – like sooty mould which makes leaves black and sticky – so many species are regarded as garden and agricultural pests.

Who Lives Under Froth?

Young garden and forest plants sometimes have patches of white froth uncannily perched in the nook of branches. Inside these messy 'homes' hide little sap-sucking bugs called spittle bugs. They are the fat nymph stage of more elongate bugs called froghoppers. The adults live outside the froth and still suck sap. Most are brown or green; some are very colourful. While the froth hides them from most predators, some birds have learnt to extract nymphs from the bubbles.

SUGAR ADDICTS

Ants love honeydew, the sweet, drug-like fluid exuded by sap-sucking hoppers and scale insects. They actually farm scale insects, even taking them back to the nest for protection at night or during winter.

The froth on this gum sapling hides a well-fed little spittle bug (below left).

True Bugs

Shield bugs may be wildly coloured and are always flat.
Inset: The stinkiest bug of all is the Spiny Black Burrowing Bug.

True bugs are so-called because they have the most classic squat, rounded bug-like shape. They differ from other bugs in that their rostrum, unlike those of other bugs, can swing out forward. Most are winged. The top wings are somewhere between hard, like a beetle's, and membranous, like a dragonfly's. They cross over the insect's back at rest. The hindwings are usually fully membranous. Although the assassin bugs are hunters, most true bugs are plant feeders that 'drink' sap through their rostrum.

Families of True Bugs

There are many families of true bugs. The plant bugs are the biggest family, with 600 species. The shield bugs make up the best known family of bugs: these flattened bugs smell bad, and some of them damage crops. There are also ground bugs. These small, elongate and usually drab-coloured bugs eat seeds. The bark or flat bugs are extremely flat and rarely seen as they emerge from under bark, yet they are widespread. Then there are the large brown crusader bugs, with a yellow cross on their backs, that live in eucalypt forests.

THE WORST SMELL

Some bugs really stink, like those green or black bugs on your backyard lemon or orange tree. But the worst smell comes from round black burrowing bugs, better known as 'stink bugs'. Their atrocious defensive smell is often released in huge quantities during spring in pasture country, when hundreds are attracted in waves to house lights. All the members of this family of true bugs dig down to attack plant roots.

Hoppers and Relatives

Horned treehoppers can have ornate headdresses larger than their bodies. Inset: Members of one family of hoppers, called fulgorids, have a long horn.

The hoppers and their relatives are a group of about 1300 species of bugs. They include tree, leaf and froghoppers. Many hoppers have bright colour patterns. The wingless nymphs come in many different shapes but the adults are elongate. Unlike true bugs, their wings usually do not cross over at rest, and their rostrums point down and back along their bodies and cannot swing forward.

Almost all hoppers are plant feeders. They often insert their rostrum directly into the plant's own sap-pumping transport system so that the plant literally pumps the sap into the insect. Much of the sap passes through undigested. Many other insects like to eat this nutritious fluid, called honeydew.

DIRTY SYRINGES

The piercing mouthparts of some species of leafhopper act like dirty syringes. While large numbers of pesky leafhoppers may cause growing plant shoots to wilt by depleting the sap, it's more sinister when some transmit viruses between plants on their mouthparts. Aphids are among the culprits.

Drummers

Some hoppers have sound-producing, or tympanal, organs similar to those of cicadas. These 'drum' skins vibrate to produce low-frequency mate-attracting sounds which we cannot hear.

Hopper Families

Froghoppers are known for their powerful jumps. Treehoppers usually live in trees and are bark-like in colour and texture. Long, flat leafhoppers live on leaves and often fly up in large numbers when you walk through grass. Another family of hoppers, called fulgorids, feature a horn-like extension on their head that makes the head almost as long as the body.

What Are the 'Portholes' on a Caterpillar For?

Look closely at a caterpillar, and you will see what look like little 'portholes' along the sides of its body. Often accentuated with colours and bold patterns, there is usually a pair on each segment. These are the spiracles through which caterpillars breathe. Spiracles are easy to see on caterpillars but on many winged insects they are hidden by the wings. The spiracles are openings into a network of tubes called trachea, which distribute oxygen to parts of the internal body cavity. The breathing system of land vertebrates like humans is different from most land insects; they use muscles to pump air in and out of that central organ known as the lungs.

Here you can see clearly the oval spiracles on every segment of the caterpillar of the large Birdwing Butterfly.

What Is a Witchetty Grub?

The term 'witchetty', roughly meaning 'hooked stick for extracting grubs', comes from a South Australian Aboriginal language. However, European Australians have borrowed the term and extended its use to refer to all bush-tucker grubs. Most witchetty grubs are arid-country caterpillars of large moths, like the goat moths, and live in roots and stems of trees. Goat moth caterpillars can grow to 8 cm long in the roots of a desert acacia. The larvae of longicorn beetles, which tunnel in living stems or in logs, are among the few edible grubs living in rainforests.

Feasting on Grubs

Ghost moth caterpillars are also referred to as witchetty grubs. One species favoured by Aborigines grows to about 13 cm long and lives in tunnels in the bark of red gums. Aborigines eat both the grubs and the adults. They catch the moths, which emerge in big numbers after rare rains, by attracting them to large fires on their first flight.

Goat moth caterpillars, like this one next to its tunnel, are the main insects now collectively called witchetty grubs.

What Is the Difference Between Butterflies and Moths?

In general butterflies are six families of day-flying moths that have attracted the attention of insect collectors. Australia has 400 species of butterflies from only five families. In comparison there are about 20 000 species of moths represented in 80 families.

Moths easily rival butterflies for colour and pattern. Their antennae taper to a point and they often rest with their wings spread.

Telltale Signs

Butterflies have thin, cylindrical antennae that end with a club-like thickening. At rest they tend to hold their wings upright and closed together. Their caterpillars vary in shape and habits but are similar to those of many moths.

The antennae of most moths taper to a point and, in males, may be feather-like in the middle. At rest, moths hold their wings either spread out flat or folded tent-like over the body.

The wings are joined by a velcro-like strip along the margins, unlike those of butterflies. Although moths' colours and patterns often rival those of butterflies, moths tend to be hairier and usually fly at night.

Butterflies, like this Red-bodied Swallowtail, rest with their wings closed. Note how their antennae thicken at the tip.

Moths and Butterflies

Looking like tiny, streamlined jet fighters, adult hawk moths can fly at 50 km per hour. Inset: A Cruiser Butterfly.

The caterpillars of the 21 000 or so species of moths and butterflies are the best known of the plant feeders. The majority chew leaves, sometimes mining inside them, curling them over or sticking them together with web. Many tunnel in living and dead trees and roots, and others eat leaf litter.

The day-flying moths and all the butterflies represent only about 5 per cent of this vast group. The colour of their wings is created by two layers of minute individual scales, ribbed like crinkle-cut chips. They vary in appearance from different angles, creating effects like the metallic colours of the Ulysses Butterfly.

Many adults get their sugars to power flight in search of a mate from nectar or fruit sap. Some adult moths do not feed at all. After mating,females lay tens to tens of thousands of eggs on leaves, twigs and bark.

Among the caterpillars are some destructive pests, like army worms, cabbage moths and clothes moths. However, most caterpillars are harmless and just get on with the job of putting on weight and size before pupating and emerging as flying adults.

THE POWER OF PERFUME

While butterflies tend to select their mates by sight, most female moths produce a pheromone odour which attracts the males under cover of darkness. The feathery antennae of many male moths have tens of thousands of sensors, finely tuned to detect individual scent molecules from over a kilometre away. Variation in the intensity of molecules hitting each antenna determines their direction.

Fruit Flies

A horde of Papaya Fruit Flies. Inset: A female fruit fly 'stinging' fruit by piercing a hole with her stiletto-like ovipositor and laying eggs.

Fruit flies are known as serious pests of fruit trees but, of approximately 140 species that are officially called fruit flies, only about 15 species are pests of commercial crops. The others are harmless and live unnoticed lives, eating rainforest fruits or seeds. Outside Australia there are other serious fruit fly pests. We need to be vigilant to ensure these don't come to our shores.

Fruit flies range from about 5 to 9 mm long and vary in colour from orange to red to black. They have beautifully patterned eyes. The males often perform dances to attract females. Females of most species inject eggs into ripening fruit using a stiletto-like extension called an ovipositor. The fruit is said to be 'stung' and shows typical spots. When the maggot larvae hatch they burrow further inwards. After as little as a week the fully grown larvae fall out of the fruit and burrow into the ground, where they pupate for 10 or more days.

Queensland Pest

The Queensland Fruit Fly uses over 100 different host plants, including most fruits, and even vegetables like pumpkins. It used to be restricted to the north but has now spread all the way to Victoria, following new cropping areas and adapting to a slower life cycle in the colder south. Strict quarantine measures have now been agreed between States.

Why Do Scientists Love Fruit Flies?

The nineteenth-century Austrian monk, Gregor Mendel, experimented with cross-breeding pea plants to understand how different characteristics, like size and colour, are inherited. He called these individual characteristics of plants 'elemente'. His meticulous work was picked up in the early twentieth century by the scientist Thomas Morgan, who experimented on a tiny fruit fly rather than pea plants. The 3 mm fly, *Drosophila melanogaster,* is known here as the Vinegar Fly. Clouds of them hover above rotting fruit, attracted to fermentation. Thomas Morgan chose them because they are easy to breed: a quarter-litre bottle can hold colonies of hundreds, which produce a new, vastly increased, generation every two weeks.

Morgan's painstaking studies showed that Mendel's 'elemente' are what we now call genes, which do indeed define the characteristics of all life. He discovered that genes live on bigger structures called chromosomes and was the first to 'map' the position of genes on these chromosomes. He was very lucky that he picked fruit flies: they have only four chromosomes, and these so huge that ordinary light microscopes can see them.

Rotting fruit is the natural habitat for the famous Vinegar Flies.

By comparison to this brilliant work, using supercomputers today to map human genes is a mere computer game.

Who Scribbled on the Scribbly Gum?

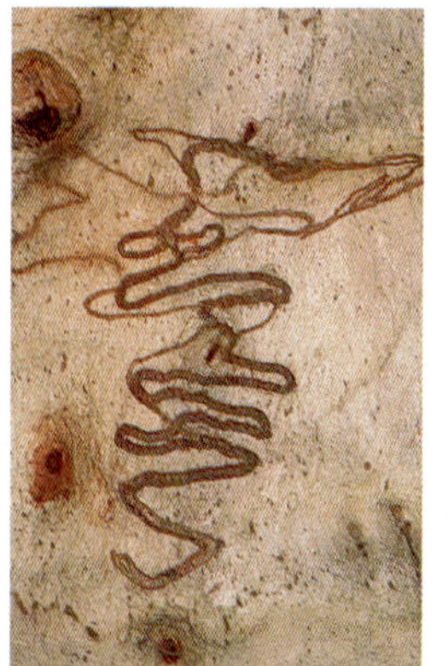

Nature's graffiti: the 'signature' of the Scribbly Gum Moth's caterpillar.

A caterpillar, would you believe. In fact the caterpillar of a small moth called the Scribbly Gum Moth. For weeks to months this caterpillar weaves crazed tunnels in the bark of several species of smooth eucalypts, including the Scribbly Gum from around Sydney's coastal region. As it mines, it feeds on the living bark. To pupate it spins a flat silk cocoon recessed into the tunnel. Adult moths have hair-fringed wings under 10 mm across.

Related caterpillars tunnel on the surface of leaves.

LOUDEST STEREO

Absolutely the loudest insect calls belong to cicadas. However, mole crickets have evolved a way to amplify their already very loud songs. They sit in a burrow with a double trumpet-shaped entrance which broadcasts in stereo up to 2 km away. Some loudspeaker designs are based on the same idea.

Who Makes the Pinholes in Timber?

Very small, very cylindrical beetles called pinhole borers. Most are less than 4 mm long and, though related to weevils, they have no snout. Adult beetles bore into living or dead wood. Instead of eating it, they infect the shavings of the sapwood with a fungus called Ambrosia Fungus. It then multiplies and becomes the beetles' main food. The beetles carry the fungus in special pits on their bodies and introduce it into the tunnels where eggs are laid. Pinhole beetle larvae chew new tunnels, but it is the fungi growing on the frass – shavings and wood dust – that they eat. Larvae pupate in the tunnels and emerge as flying adults after a year or two, leaving a telltale pile of sawdust near the pinhole.

The tiny legs and cylindrical bodies of pinhole beetles fit perfectly into their neat tunnels.

What Are Weevils?

Weevils are beetles. They are recognisable by their long 'snouts'. They are the most diverse organisms on the planet. Over 8000 species, from 1 to 65 mm long, have been named in Australia alone, with a known world total of over 45 000.

The 'snout'is an extension of the head and may be longer than the body. Known as a rostrum, it has jaws at the tip and antennae with a distinct elbow mounted halfway along. It uses its rostrum to bore thin holes in wood or seeds into which it safely hides its egg.

Most weevils have a stout body armour and are a dull colour but a few are bright green or blue. Their fat, curved, white, grub-like larvae feed inside wood, roots and especially seeds. They take from several months to a year or two to develop.

While some weevils are famous pests of crops, like the rice and grain weevils and the Cotton Boll Weevil, most go about their business unnoticed. Among school kids a few of the larger species (2–3 cm) are sometimes known as 'splinter pullers' as their small but strong jaws can grip small objects with surprising force.

DEATH KNOCKS

Some beetles live in tunnels all their lives. To find each other they knock on the tunnel walls. These sounds are so loud they can be heard outside the wood. Chair-bound people, alarmed by the incessant knocking of 'deathwatch' beetles, imagined these sounds to herald death.

There are more species of weevil than any other known creature.

Wood Borers

The antennae of a longicorn beetle are typically longer than its body. Inset: Their larvae may tunnel in trees for several years.

The larvae of thousands of beetle species, several families of moths and the odd wasp burrow inside trees. The best known wood borers are the longicorn or long-horned beetles, and the showy jewel beetles.

Most select damaged trees for homes. Others cause damage to permit entry of their larvae. For example, some longicorn beetles ringbark branches with their mandibles before laying eggs. While beetle larvae pupate in the tunnels, moth larvae often fall to the ground to pupate.

FIREBUGS

Certain species of jewel beetles are strangely attracted to campfires. This odd behaviour is no accident but an ingenious use of infrared sensors to seek bushfires. In areas affected by bushfires, these beetles find the sort of bark damage they need to lay their eggs in. While some wait until the fire dies down, others risk their lives to lay their eggs in the cracks the fire opens while it still rages.

Diet and Nature's Cycle

Many larvae carry bacteria in their gut to help them digest the cellulose and lignin in wood. Some beetles even make their own potent digestive enzymes. Nevertheless, wood is poor food and that is why many larvae take two or more years to reach maturity.

Tunnels made by wood borers provide access to a succession of other insects, fungi and bacteria. A cycle of invaders may eventually kill and decompose a tree. Soggy rainforest logs are filled with larvae, especially those of scarab, stag and darkling beetles.

Sawflies

Sawflies are not related to flies, but are a group of primitive wasps best known for their colourful and destructive larvae. Unlike typical wasps such as paper wasps, adult sawflies have no visible 'waist' between the abdomen and thorax, and no sting. The name 'sawfly' is derived from their short but very stout and serrated egg-laying ovipositor, which they use to 'saw' into leaves and wood to deposit eggs out of harm's way.

The larvae are caterpillar-like, with six pointed legs. They sometimes have little stubby 'prolegs' on the abdominal segments. Some live inside wood, others mine inside leaves or make galls – tumour-like growths on leaves – in which to lay their eggs. The majority of species are conspicuous, living in close masses on leaves.

'Spitfire' grubs ready to squirt foul fluids at an attacker. Inset: Typical adult sawfly without a wasp 'waist'.

THE FIRST VELCRO

Most flying insects have four wings. The best acrobats, like dragonflies, can beat the two pairs independently giving greater agility. But many insects use both pairs together for simpler but energy-efficient flight. Wasps and sawflies join the two pairs using a mechanism that looks and works like a zipper. Moths evolved a velcro-like join about 150 million years before we reinvented it.

Spitfires

Gardeners know some sawflies as 'spitfires'. These gaudy larvae gather in writhing masses during the day and defend themselves by spitting foul chemicals, derived from the oil concentrates of food plants, often eucalypts. Cattle accidentally eating them with foliage have been known to be poisoned. At night the grubs split up and feed on leaves high in the tree but they regroup each day for protection. They drop and burrow into the soil to pupate, sometimes emerging over two seasons to maximise their chance of finding sufficient quality food.

Scavengers

Who Are the Scavengers?

In arid Australia meat ants – seen here disposing of a dead mouse – are among the most efficient scavengers.

Animals that eat the flesh of dead creatures, the 'vultures' of the world, are traditionally referred to as scavengers. Saprophagy describes the practice of eating decaying plant material. Both behaviours exist among insects but for the sake of simplicity the word scavenger will be used here to describe them all.

The majority of fly larvae eat decaying matter, preferring the wetter stuff, like flesh, excrement and wet humus. Many insects, from tiny springtails to cockroaches, crickets and beetles, eat leaf litter. Beetle and moth larvae voraciously attack dead wood. Most scavengers have a varied diet but there are some famous specialists, like the dung beetles that feed on the dung of just one species of mammal. The rubbish in birds' nests also supports communities of insects like moth and beetle larvae that feed on dung, feathers and the birds' food. Nothing in nature goes to waste.

Why Are Scavengers So Important?

Nutrients like nitrogen are the building blocks of life. Without them there would be no more new plants or animals. These must be recycled, and this process is driven by scavengers.

Although the main decomposers of plant matter are fungi, followed by bacteria, the role of insects – small as they are – is essential. The decomposing action is started and speeded up by the chewing and turning-over activities of insects. They also transport fungal spores and bacteria to where they are needed. Wood-boring insects introduce fungi and other decomposers to more surface areas of wood. Termites even carry bacteria in their gut to help with digesting wood, which has mutual advantages: the termites get more energy from their food, and the bacteria get fed and housed. Dung eaters are especially important, as once dung dries in the sun, the nutrients locked up inside are hard to recycle into the soil. The chewing and burying actions of the dung beetles therefore improve the soil.

Darkling beetles are important decomposers of dead wood and other plant matter. This one is carrying a hitchhiking mite.

Why Are There So Many Flies?

Within hours of a kangaroo dying nearby, thousands of blowflies arrive and cover the plants and ground around it.

Before Europeans brought houseflies to Australia, Bush Flies were the dominant flies on this dry continent. They buzz around animals and humans seeking body moisture to drink and protein to make more flies with. The explorers Burke and Wills coined the phrase 'sticky flies' during their travels.

Bush Flies must lay their eggs in fresh dung before it dries out. One female can lay up to 1000 eggs. These hatch into larvae – known as maggots – and pupate into adults, all in around four to five days. If the food is running out they can develop faster and hatch in three days as smaller adults. The presence of domestic animals has increased their food supply and competing insects, like dung beetles, are not always in the right place at the right time due to their slower breeding rate and aversion to aridity. This gives flies a staggering numerical advantage, a thousand-fold increase every four days or so! Houseflies and blowflies have similar cycles, but while housefly larvae eat almost anything, blowfly larvae eat only flesh.

What Are Maggots?

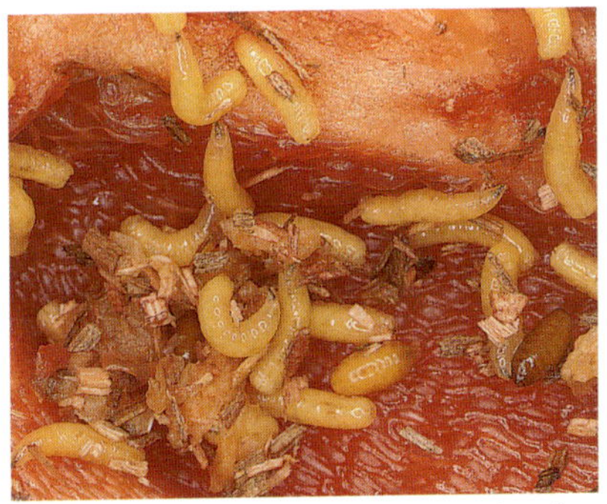

Maggots are usually gregarious, like these fruit fly larvae devouring a capsicum.

Insects which undergo complete metamorphosis grow from egg to larvae to pupa to adult. Butterfly larvae are called caterpillars and the larvae of many other insects are simply called grubs. The name maggot is given to the larvae of true flies (see page 74), like houseflies, blowflies and march flies.

Maggots vary in shape, depending on the habits of the particular species. In general they are simple white grubs, often tapering at both ends. Their lives are usually spent in wet and mucky surroundings where wriggling about and eating are the main activities. This explains why most maggots lack legs and eyes. The majority of them feed on rotting organic matter but there are such animals as predatory maggots that hunt other live soft maggoty morsels.

True Flies

Male Stalk-eyed Flies use their antler-like eyes in courtship battles. Inset: Houseflies sponge up sweat for moisture and protein.

The word 'fly' is used for a myriad of insects but true flies are a very distinct group, all characterised by having only one pair of wings. The second pair has evolved into small, club-like counterbalancing appendages which increase flying agility. Of the 8000-odd species in Australia some, like the mosquitoes and midges, are long-antennaed primitive flies, while those with the typical housefly or march fly shape have short-antennae and make up the majority of species.

Fly larvae are known as maggots and most live in rotting habitats, from mud, compost and dung to the bottoms of ponds, where they contribute to recycling nutrients. Parasitic fly maggots live inside other insect larvae and pupae. Most adult flies pollinate flowers; some carnivorous groups hunt other flies. Most flies are beneficial. Their reputation is marred by biting flies like mosquitoes and sandflies, which need animal blood to develop their eggs, and by the few destructive flies that attack living flesh, like the Sheep Blowfly.

YOU'RE STANDING IN IT

Most insects smell with their antennae and taste with their mouthparts but some moths, butterflies and flies taste with the hairs on their 'feet'. This makes searching for food faster and safer. They just land briefly on potential food to check it out.

Houseflies

A tolerance of low light and a broad diet allows houseflies to thrive in houses. Like most flies, they smother their food with digestive enzymes, then mop up the liquified mess with sponge-like mouthparts. By moving from dirty to clean areas, they can transmit diseases.

Cockroaches

The Giant Burrowing Cockroach is a gentle non-smelly species that lives in family groups. Inset: This brightly coloured roach does smell.

This is probably the most disliked insect on the planet but its bad reputation is based on less than 10 species out of about 4000. Australia is home to around 400 species. Ten are known to be introduced.

Habits and Life Cycle

Most cockroaches do not live in peoples' homes. They occupy many places and scavenge on plant detritus, thereby playing an important role in the recycling of nutrients in the environment. During the day their flat, slippery bodies allow them to hide in crevices, under bark or under stones. The few species active during the day tend to warn off predators with bright colours and defend themselves against attack with foul secretions.

Females make a flat leathery case called an ootheca into which they lay 10–40 eggs. A few species have live young. There is no larval stage, only a series of nymphs that look like miniature adults without wings. In the tropics there may be several generations a year but in colder parts development takes a year or more.

House Guests

One reason for the spectacular success of the few domestic species is that they eat almost any organic material, a rare habit among insects. The American Cockroach, the most successful of the house guests, can live up to four years. It inhabits almost exclusively houses and drains, where its speed and acute warning senses make it hard to eradicate. It can pick up vibrations as small as one millionth of a millimetre, and sprint off at the second fastest recorded insect running speed of 8.9 km per hour.

Do Carpet Beetles Eat Carpet?

The blotchy pattern on these adult carpet beetles is characteristic of this family.

Yes, but they are choosy. Animal fur and wool are tasty morsels for the beetles' distinctive fat, hairy larvae. Provided it is made of natural fibres like wool, they could infest your carpet but nylon carpets have no appeal.

Carpet beetles belong to a family of scavenging beetles. Many of them feed on dry carcasses and are known as hide beetles. Some eat only the cast-off skins of other insects, breaking down the tough exoskeleton proteins. There are even species that steal the dry remnant husks of insects in spider webs. Others have the rare skill, shared with the feared clothes moths, of being able to break down keratin – the protein that makes hair and feathers so tough.

Furniture and Feathers

Feather-eating carpet beetles often live in bird nests. They were also fond of feather pillows and mattresses when these were popular. In the old days, horse-hair-filled sofas provided a comfortable nest for beetle larvae; one old home manual recommended soaking infested sofas in petrol!

Adult carpet beetles are flat, oval-shaped and often patterned with multicoloured flecks that come off on your hands and make the beetles slippery. Unlike their larvae, they feed in flowers.

The stumpy, bristle-haired larvae of carpet beetles are unmistakable.

JOBS FOR BEETLES

The bad habits of some hide beetles are put to good use in museums. The efficient 'museum' beetle strips dry carcasses down to their skeletons, ready for display. They are bred specifically for that purpose but must be strictly confined as their break-out would cause chaos among displays that possess skin, hair and feathers. A relative of this species is considered the scourge of insect collections, reducing many to dust.

Are Cockroaches Really Dirty?

All insects are fastidious about their bodies. Even in the dirtiest habitats insects are rarely covered in muck or even dust. This is because most of their sense organs – fine hairs or sensory pits – are external and mounted on the exoskeleton or antennae. To keep these in perfect working order, they clean all parts of their bodies, often with special combs and tools on their legs. Most cockroaches live in the wild and rarely have anything worse than dust to contend with. However, pest cockroach species which share places with humans sometimes hide in very dark and dank places of our making – like sewers. It is therefore possible for them to carry bacteria on their feet and antennae, while their bodies are shiny clean. The American Cockroach, also found here, has been reported to carry salmonella bacteria, which can cause serious gastric infections in crowded cities. The same cockroaches in a country house are less likely to carry anything dangerous.

The widespread 'Australian' Cockroach is the most likely species to be wandering over your food at night.

Do Roaches Make Good Pets?

The largest cockroach in the world is a native Australian. The wingless Giant Burrowing Cockroach grows to 80 mm long and weighs up to 35 g. Some small, furry mammals, like bats, weigh only 4 g. This huge roach lives in northern Queensland in long underground tunnels, where females care for their young, bringing dead leaves down for the nymphs to feed on. Through the pet trade these monsters are helping reverse the public revulsion towards cockroaches. Observing them in sandy aquariums has become very popular. A roach family will establish tunnels and live much like ants on an ant farm for the education and enjoyment of their human carers. They are not oily like some roaches, move slowly and do not seem to mind being handled.

The Giant Burrowing Cockroach is a handful and adapts well to domesticity.

Dung Beetles

A native dung beetle burrowing through fresh horse dung. Inset: Only a few Australian species roll perfect balls of dung.

Dung beetles were worshipped in ancient Egypt and are well known all over the world. They perform the important job of recycling nutrients back into the soil by burying dung and leaf litter. Elephant dung beetles in Africa are over 65 mm long, but as we have no really large native herbivores in Australia, our dung beetles tend to be small and less apparent. Most local species are under 12 mm.

Recycling Roo Poo

About 300 Australian species bury the dung of native animals and some feed on leaf litter and fungi. Because pellets of kangaroo and wallaby dung are small and often far apart, some specialist dung beetles use claws to grip the fur around a kangaroo's anus and ride along waiting for a dropping, onto which they bail out.

Most bury the dung where it falls, sometimes in elaborate tunnels with side galleries, where each c-shaped larva feeds on its very own prepared ball of dung. With such parental care the larvae grow quickly, often pupating after only a month.

Some species make dung balls bigger than themselves and roll them away backwards to bury elsewhere. Males and females cooperate in forming balls and stashing them away, but the balls for feeding the larvae are usually only handled by females.

DUNG DILEMMA

With the introduction of cattle and horses into Australia, native dung beetles were overwhelmed. Big piles of unburied dung bred pesky bush flies. To help with its burial, African and Mediterranean dung beetles have been a successful import.

Burying Beetles

A burying beetle wanders over a carcass, inspecting it before attempting to bury it.

Many insects and other invertebrates take part in the essential task of recycling dead animals in the environment. Fly maggots and many types of beetles are involved at different stages of decomposition. The most fascinating specialists are the large, flat burying beetles. There are only three local species and most eat dead vertebrates like mice, birds or frogs. Often a male will arrive first, attracted by the smell. He will then use pheromones to attract a female. If many beetles arrive, fighting ensues until one couple claims the prize. They cooperate in digging a chamber under the carcass into which it slowly sinks.

Parental Care

Some species stay together in pairs to rear the young but more often the female chases the male off when the carcass has been cleaned and prodded into a well-buried sphere. The female stays in the chamber, lays eggs near the ball and softens a part of it with digestive fluids. When the larvae hatch she attracts their attention with sounds, made by rubbing body parts together. This causes them to crane their bodies like baby birds in a nest. She feeds them individually until they are big enough to burrow into the ball. With such rich protein food their growth is phenomenal: they double in size in the first seven hours, and within seven days are 100 times heavier and ready to pupate.

Can Insects Starve Out Us Humans?

An infestation of flour beetles attacking stored wheat.

Humans eat a very small proportion of the possible foods on this planet. Most of our needs are met by about twenty species of plants and domesticated animals, so most insects' habits do not interfere with us. However, among those that do share our foods are some very persistent competitors. Monoculture – the growing of a single crop in one area – causes huge build-ups of plant-eating insects on farms. In storage areas, grains and fruits attract specialist beetles that humans inadvertently spread around the world.

Historical Damage and New Protections

The Romans wrote about devastation of grain stocks by weevils. Weevils, too, ate the wheat destined for Australia on the First Fleet, causing much initial hardship. Colorado Potato Beetles have devastated potato crops of whole countries, while plague locusts still cause massive seasonal crop damage, especially in Africa.

In the past century the use of insecticides has limited attacks, but at an enormous environmental cost. Today better storage methods and the use of carbon dioxide and heat treatments that kill insects are superseding poisons for stored crops in the West but crops in the developing world are still under great threat.

DRIEST DESERT

Insects that live in deserts get water from dry plants, rare dew and occasional rain. Grain silos must be kept drier than the driest deserts but even in this parched environment specialist grain beetles have adapted by retaining the liquid by-product from the burning of carbohydrates, which other animals expel.

Rice weevils attacking stored rice

Do Earwigs Live in Ears?

The simple answer is no. However, even though there is no real evidence that they crawl into ears, when people slept closer to the ground earwigs may well have accidentally wound up exploring clothing or indeed ears, sparking the odd anecdote.

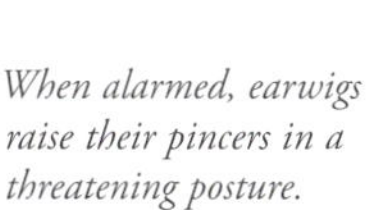

When alarmed, earwigs raise their pincers in a threatening posture.

Ear Wings

These nocturnal roaming insects have a pair of pincer-like forceps at the rear, and small wing cases that hide a set of very cleverly folded large wings. The origami-like folding pattern is so complex that the insect sometimes needs to use its legs or even pincers to help furl or unfurl them. The wings are vaguely ear shaped and one theory claims that the name stems from this resemblance and evolved from the name 'ear wing'. Another theory is that the pincers resemble an instrument once used to pierce ears for earrings.

Behaviour

Earwigs are familiar to gardeners because of an introduced European species which is now established enough to be a pest. Most of the 60 Australian species are shy nocturnal insects that eat mainly dead plant and animal matter; some also hunt other insects. The pincers are often raised in a defensive display, as well as being used for hunting and holding prey, and in ritual courting displays. Earwigs rarely bite people and their bite is not painful.

The Gum Tree Earwig is a common hunter under tree bark but rarely found anywhere near ears.

MATERNAL TO A FAULT

The earwig is one of the rare insects that cares for its young. Females clean the eggs and feed the young nymphs. However, the nymphs need to moult four or five times to become adults and, if they remain in their mother's burrow beyond the second moult, she may eat them. For one European species this pattern is reversed: the female, weak from rearing the nymphs, dies in the nest and becomes their food.

Parasites and Pests

What Is a Parasite?

A parasite is an organism which derives all its needs from another, larger organism known as a host. The host gets no benefit from this relationship. Classic examples of insect parasites are ticks, lice and fleas, which feed on the blood of mammals and birds. It is not in the interest of a parasite to kill its host as that would reduce the availablity of future generations for the parasite to feed on.

Some parasitic wasps can 'smell' fruit fly eggs inside fruit, and parasitise them with their own eggs.

Parasitoids

There are also many species of wasps and flies that are halfway between predators and parasites. These are known as parasitoids. They often paralyse other insects before laying their eggs on them, and their larvae eat the immobilised living insect. More insect larvae, eggs and sometimes adults are killed this way than by all other types of predators combined.

Biters

The biting flies like mosquitoes and march flies are not actually parasites but, because some carry parasites, and all bite and bother us, the scope of this chapter includes these pesky insects.

Are There Parasites on Parasites?

This 3 mm wasp parasitises the eggs of other parasitic insects.

Parasitism is often more complex than simply one parasite attacking a host. Parasites attack other parasites and parasitoids attack other parasitoids. For example, some parasitic flies chase parasitic wasps and lay an egg on them in flight. Cuckoo wasps invade nests of parasitic wasps and parasitise their larvae.

But the most improbable example must be the small wasps of one bizarre little family whose larvae parasitise the larvae of other parasitic wasps growing inside the same caterpillar host. The female wasps lay thousands of eggs on leaves that moth caterpillars eat. But the caterpillars may also have other parasite eggs inside them. The eggs of both parasites hatch inside the caterpillars. The wasp larvae feed on the caterpillar, but in order to fully develop, they also need to eat the parasitic larvae of the other species present.

What Is Malaria?

Malaria is not caused by a virus or a bacteria, but by a single-celled protozoan parasite from the genus *Plasmodium*, commonly called the Malaria Parasite. It is finely tuned for a life cycle involving mosquitoes and humans. Some species of the tropical mosquito genus *Anopheles*, known as malaria mosquitoes, carry the protozoa, which escapes digestion in the stomach by migrating to the salivary glands.

From here it passes to the next human the mosquito bites. The protozoa moves into the human's liver, where it multiplies for one or two weeks before changing form and migrating into the blood. There it attacks red blood cells, rupturing them as it multiplies itself. At this stage, weakened by anaemia from a lowered red-blood cell count, people experience the characteristic high fever of malaria. While continuing to multiply, the protozoa produces a reproductive stage that is then picked up by another mosquito, and the cycle continues.

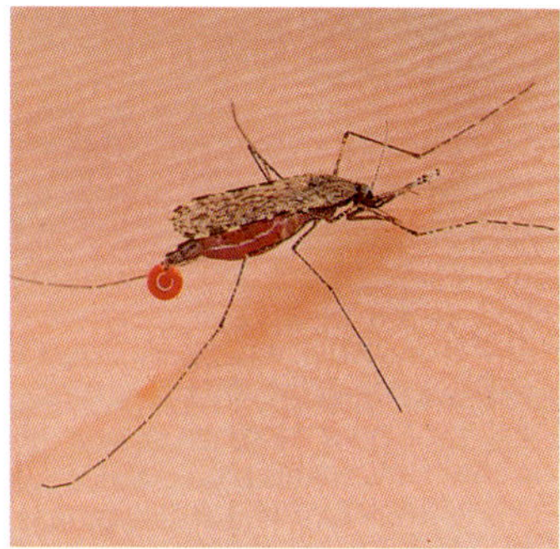

The Australian Malaria Mosquito is not dangerous as long as malaria is absent here.

Why Is Malaria So Dangerous?

Worldwide two to three million people die each year from malaria. A hundred times as many contract it, largely in Africa where a very human-oriented species of mosquito is the main carrier. Since World War II the United Nations has run major schemes combining the use of insecticides and preventive medicines to alleviate the situation. These worked wonders until the 1960s. However, increasing resistance of mosquitoes to insecticides, and of *Plasmodium* to the main medicine, combined with unstable politics in affected areas, started to reverse the gains.

The most deadly strain of the parasite, *Plasmodium falciparum*, attacks the brain and is known as Cerebral Malaria. This strain is now the most resistant to the safer and cheaper drug treatments. The less-safe pesticide DDT, now banned in most countries, was one of the best tools, reducing the total number of cases in Sri Lanka from 3.5 million cases in 1940 to five in 1962. Agricultural use of DDT led to major environmental damage and huge insect-resistance problems, but controlled use in homes overseas was still effective against malaria, and considered reasonably safe until the 1990s, when it was banned.

ALL SAFE NOW?

Through the great efforts of its health authorities, Australia managed to eradicate endemic malaria by 1981. Hundreds of cases a year are still reported but these are all acquired overseas. Since the deadly *falciparum* strain lurks as close as New Guinea, it's vital that travellers seek medical advice and take precautions.

Mosquitoes

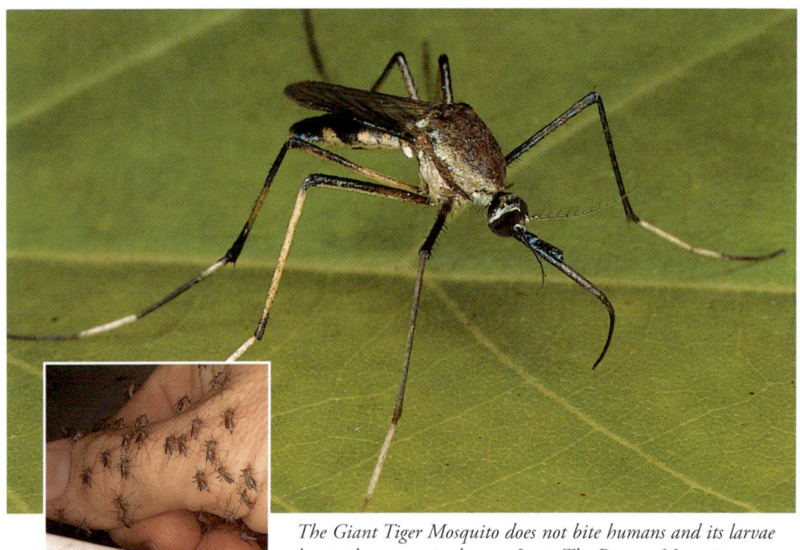

The Giant Tiger Mosquito does not bite humans and its larvae hunt other mosquito larvae. Inset: The Dengue Mosquito.

There are around 300 species of mosquitoes in Australia, from the cold mountains of Tasmania to the hot, dank, salty swamps of Cape York. All have aquatic larvae that like slow-flowing rivers, lakes, mangrove swamps, puddles and containers like tin cans. The mosquito that carries dengue fever prefers breeding in small containers and lives around dwellings in northern Australia. A few other species carry parasites and viruses, like malaria, encephalitis and Ross River fever.

Adult males have furry antennae and feed on nectar to fuel their flight. Only female mosquitoes bite, as they need the blood for protein to produce eggs. Attracted by carbon dioxide, a by-product of breathing air, they will bite most animals, including humans. The anti-coagulant chemicals in female mosquito saliva cause the itching and swelling allergic reaction when they bite.

Mating and Life Cycle

Mosquitoes mate in flight. Males are drawn to the annoying whine of the female's wings. The females deposit eggs on the water or the bank. The wriggler larvae live a week or so, coming to the surface to breathe through a siphon. Unusually, mosquito pupae are active swimmers and float to the surface for the adults to emerge.

GOURMET MOSSIES

Different species prefer odours of different body parts. Some mossies love noses. The ankle-biters like smelly feet. In one experiment they were drawn to a substitute of limberger cheese, which is said to smell like sweaty feet.

March Flies

The painful bite of a march fly is caused by its large, rasping proboscis, designed to penetrate the thick hides of animals like horses.

Most people have experienced the painful bites of march flies but not all of the 250 species bite humans, as their other common name, horse flies, attests. However, the many species that do bite people often hatch in population waves that make some parts of the country unbearable in spring and summer.

Attractive Smells and Painful Bites

March flies have large heads and huge eyes with up to tens of thousands of individual facets. However, they do not use eyesight to find their victims. Instead, they are attracted to the carbon dioxide humans and other animals exhale. As a fly gets closer to its target it is drawn by other cues like body heat and odours, and apparently dark colours. Like mosquitoes, only females bite as they need protein from blood for egg development. These they lay in damp places. The maggots feed and pupate, emerging as weather warms up.

March fly bites hurt more than mosquito bites because march flies use large, wide, rasping mouthparts suitable for biting through thicker hides than ours. An allergic reaction to their saliva causes varying degrees of itch. No known human diseases are carried by march flies in Australia. However, in Africa they sometimes carry dangerous parasites.

THE FASTEST FLIGHT

Since 1917 a dragonfly has held the record, at 98 km per hour for a downhill flight. But in 1984 hovering male march flies, using a particular manoeuvre on spotting mates, were found to accelerate to 145 km per hour for just an instant!

What Are Bed Bugs?

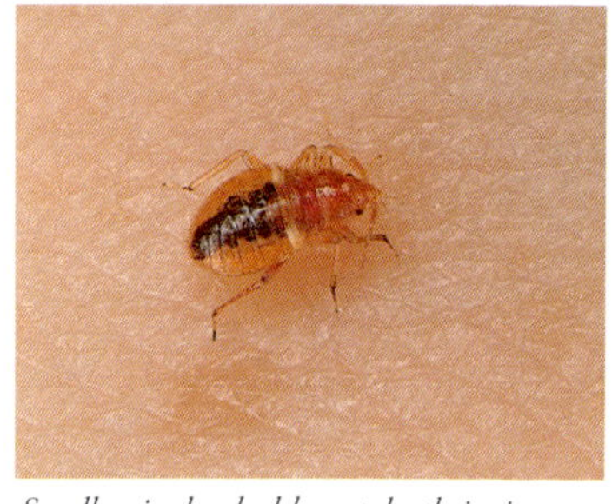

Small, wingless bed bugs take their time exploring the body before biting.

Bed bugs in Australia belong to a single worldwide species of wingless sucking bug, with a very flat, round body 5–8 mm long. Now almost exclusively domestic, by day they hide in crevices in the room, emerging at night to feed on human blood. In a room full of people, a greedy bed bug will return to the same victim every night, even though a full blood meal could sustain it for weeks.

A variation in air temperature of only 1°C triggers a homing instinct to a bug's particular prey. So far, in Australia, no dangerous diseases are known to be transmitted by bed bugs.

Why Are Insects So Hard To Eradicate?

Insects do well on this planet for several reasons. Their tough exoskeleton assists in their survival. The fact that most can fly makes it easy for them to spread to new areas which they can rapidly populate. The fecundity of insects is staggering. Not only do the females of many species lay thousands of eggs each but new generations may appear every few weeks, continuously multiplying this effect. A breeding pair of houseflies, with no predators and infinite resources, can theoretically breed up a sphere of flies 93 million miles across in just one year! This rapid turnover of generations also leads to production of more new genetic combinations, resulting in mutations that have resistance to our insecticides in the same way that they have already developed resistance to the chemical warfare waged on them by their food plants.

Human Factors in Insect Success

More and more people are opposed to causing the extinction of other species sharing this planet. There are also good ecological reasons for not deliberately tinkering with the balance of the ecosystem. Despite this, people have tried very hard to eradicate insects but with only a few 'successes' in small areas like islands. The destruction of habitats indiscriminately eradicates many species, while crop pests continue to prosper. This is because planting single-species crops encourages populations, while their natural enemies 'accidentally' lose their homes and fall victim to our persistent use of pesticides.

Moth eggs. Large numbers of eggs aid insect survival.

What Are Sandflies?

The term sandflies refers to any number of very small, biting flies related to midges and mosquitoes. The name originally belongs to a genus of minute flies in the Middle East, species of which are found here but rarely interact with people. Strictly speaking, the famous Australian sandflies common in tidal areas like beaches and mangroves are known as 'biting midges'; in America they go by the very apt name of 'no-see-ums'.

Sandflies produce many generations in one season. Their larvae live in the rich mud of the tidal zone. The adults are only about 2 mm across and the females need to feed on blood to produce the next brood. Although they are known to spread various viruses and parasites elsewhere in the world, in Australia they are just extremely annoying and their bites cause allergic reactions with persistent itching.

Although minute, sandflies pack a big bite.

Can Beetles Be Parasites?

The short answer is yes. While many beetles fall prey to parasitoids when they are larvae, a few beetle families also have parasitic habits. The strange larvae of colourful, often poisonous blister beetles have extra claws for gripping fine hair. They wait patiently on flowers and hitch a ride on bees back to the hive, where they consume the bee larvae. Another beetle group uses the same strategy with various wasps, eating the parasitic wasp larvae in their nests. Even baby cockroaches are attacked this way by Fan Beetle larvae. Fly pupae are the target of parasitoid rove beetle larvae which feed slowly at first so as not to kill and spoil their food source.

Blister beetles grab a pollen meal from flowers, leaving behind larvae which wait for bees that they then parasitise.

Fleas

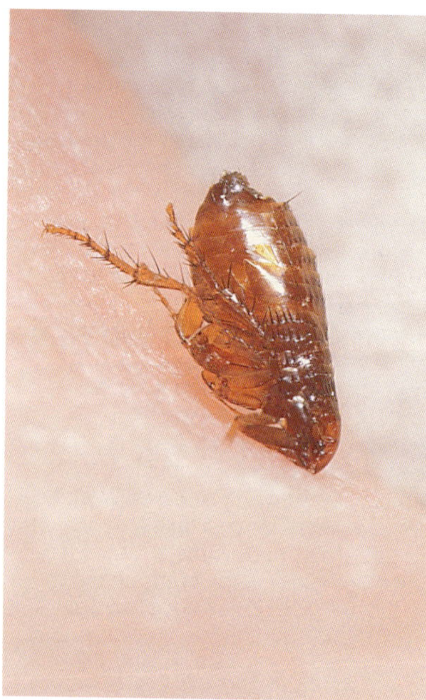

Fleas use a hammer-like mechanism to break through the skin when biting.

Fleas are parasites of nesting animals. Unlike lice, which live out their life cycle on their hosts, flea larvae, and sometimes adults, live among the detritus of their nest or burrow, only hopping on a host at meal times. This ability to move between animals helps them to survive lean times. They are attracted to their hosts by the warm carbon dioxide they exhale. They catapult themselves between passing animals by amazing jumps.

Behaviour and Life Cycle

Many mammals and a few birds carry fleas, which feed on their blood. They do not simply insert tube-like mouthparts into their hosts, but have a hammer-like mechanism that helps them rapidly penetrate through the skin to a capillary. The larvae feed on skin flakes and other refuse, and on undigested blood in the adults' droppings. Fleas pupate in the nest and can postpone hatching until a host arrives.

Fleas and Disease

One species of flea specialises in humans – the so-called Human Flea – but most fleas easily switch hosts, so we are also bitten by cat, dog, rat and other fleas.

Rats have been recorded as carriers of up to 22 different species of fleas. This makes fleas potentially dangerous carriers of disease and parasites. The Oriental Rat Flea still causes outbreaks of the plague or 'Black Death' of medieval fame in other parts of the world.

In Australia fleas can transmit to humans a dangerous disease called murine typhus and several parasites. They have also been used to transmit myxomatosis between rabbits.

FLYING LEAP

A 3 mm Cat Flea can jump 340 mm, accelerating so fast it feels the force of gravity 60 times over in a split second. A human would be well and truly squished to a pulp by such acceleration. Flea leg muscles are made of an elastic protein called resilin which can release 97 per cent of stored energy. When preparing to jump, the tensing muscles compress the flea, while body plates lock it together like a ratchet. To jump it releases the locks and the stored energy.

Lice and 'Crabs'

The Human Head Louse glues its eggs onto hair; they are impossible to comb out. Inset: The infamous Human 'Crab' Louse has big claws for clinging to pubic hair.

Of the 255 species of lice in Australia only three interact with humans. Lice are very specific to only one host species. More than half of all lice live on birds, many on marsupials, and some arrived with introduced domestic and farm animals.

Description

All lice share a similar specialised body shape. They have a flattened, wingless, hard body. Their claw-like feet, used for gripping hair and feathers, vary between species but even the claws on individuals can differ from one foot to another. Most bird lice have chewing mouthparts. Mammalian lice have sucking mouthparts with a stumpy beak, hiding sharp needles for piercing skin.

Reproduction and Habits

Reproduction is similar for most species. The Human Head Louse lays up to 10 eggs a day for up to 30 days. An elaborate cement is used to attach the eggs to hair and feathers, making it impossible for the host to dislodge them. Eggs hatch about two weeks later and the nymphs look like small adults. Bird lice feed on feathers and skin flakes; some mammalian lice also feed on dead skin. The sucking lice feed on blood, which makes them potential carriers of disease. Despite being the origin of the term 'feeling lousy', in Australia the Human Head Louse and the Human 'Crab' Louse have not been associated with serious diseases since colonial times.

THE COLDEST INSECT

The Weddell Seal Louse lives a life on the edge. Too cold to move, it clings to the fur as the seal hunts in the salty –2°C Antarctic waters, absorbing oxygen directly from the water. As the seal warms up from swimming, the louse becomes active for long enough to feed. However, to reproduce it has to wait till the seal goes onshore in its breeding season.

Parasitic Wasps

Spider wasps paralyse spiders. Inset: This small wasp has just emerged from the white pupal case of a case moth.

Over half the wasp families have parasitic habits. Because their larvae usually kill hosts rather than simply feed on them, they are known as parasitoids. Most at risk are the larvae of moths, butterflies and beetles, but grasshoppers, bugs and spiders are also targets. The wasps use smell sensors on their antennae to find hosts, homing in first on hosts' food plants, then on specifics, like their droppings or even saliva.

Some wasp parasites lay thousands of eggs in the path of ants. Larvae hatch and latch onto passing ants, riding unnoticed back to the nest where they eat the ant larvae. Most parasitic wasps lay eggs with their long egg-laying tubes (ovipositors) directly into or onto hosts' larvae or eggs. Some use these to probe into tree branches and inject their eggs into wood-boring larvae deep within. The wasp larvae slowly eat the growing host, which usually dies before pupating.

Spider-hunting parasitic wasps engender such panic that spiders rarely fight back before being stung, paralysed, taken to burrows and slowly eaten alive by the larvae.

PERFECT MEMORY

Many parasitoid wasps deposit paralysed prey in burrows. Even after long hunting flights they can find their way back to the burrow using their perfect picture memory of the location of objects around it. If anything is moved, they can no longer find their way home. To test this, scientists rearranged pebbles and even whole artificial trees around burrows, confusing the wasps.

Parasitic Flies

This large Emperor Gum Moth caterpillar has tiny parasitoid fly eggs laid on its body. Inset: Maggots emerging from a butterfly's dead pupa.

There are many flies of both parasitic and parasitoid habit (see page 84). Among the parasites are serious livestock pests like louse flies, keds and screw worm flies (not yet in Australia), the maggots of which feed on the flesh of mammals and birds. A 'fly-blown' sheep is the victim of a species of blowfly. One family of wingless flies lives only on bats. Even frogs have fly parasites. Remarkably, some of these flies give birth to live young.

The Parasitoids

Parasitoid fly species are more common. They attack other insects, especially the caterpillars of butterflies and moths and larvae of beetles. Grasshoppers, bugs and even earthworms and spiders may carry them. The maggots of one group of about 600 species feeds inside caterpillars, leaving their vital organs until last to maintain their walking larder. Their tiny white eggs can be seen on the outside of hapless caterpillars. Other families parasitise the eggs and larvae of flies and wasps, sometimes of other parasitoids. Larvae of the handsome hovering bee flies eat grasshopper eggs.

NOT ALL BAD

Most parasitic flies are best described as beneficial. Their voracious larvae eat up huge numbers of insects, many of which are garden and farm pests. Even locusts do not escape their attention. As they rampage through our crops, they are often being devoured from the inside by parasitic flies.

A Checklist of Australian Insect Groups

The following is a list of the 25 orders of insects found in Australia. These comprise over 600 often obscure families. Only those insect families discussed in this book are listed here. Others you will find in more technical books.

	Silverfish –	**Order Zygentoma**
	Bristletails –	**Order Archaeognatha**
	Mayflies –	**Order Ephemeroptera**
	Dragonflies and Damselflies –	**Order Odonata**
	Stoneflies –	**Order Plecoptera**
	Cockroaches and Termites –	**Order Blattodea**
	Praying Mantids –	**Order Mantodea**
	Earwigs –	**Order Dermaptera**
	Crickets and Grasshoppers –	**Order Orthoptera**
	Locusts and Grasshoppers –	Family Acrididae
	Pygmy Grasshoppers –	Family Tetrigidae
	Monkey Grasshoppers –	Family Eumastacidae
	Mole Crickets –	Family Gryllotalpidae
	King Crickets –	Family Stenopelmatidae
	Katydids –	Family Tettigoniidae
	Stick and Leaf Insects –	**Order Phasmatodea**
	Embiids or Web-spinners –	**Order Embioptera**
	Booklice, Psocids and Lice –	**Order Psocoptera**
	Bugs, including Hoppers, Cicadas, Scale Insects and others –	**Order Hemiptera**
Soft Bugs	Aphids –	Family Aphididae
	Scale Insects –	Families Coccidae, Margarodidae, Diaspididae and others
	Mealy Bugs –	Family Margarodidae
Hoppers	Spittle Bugs and Froghoppers –	Families Cercopidae and Aphrophoridae
	Cicadas –	Family Cicadidae
	Leafhoppers –	Family Cicadellidae
	Treehoppers –	Family Membracidae
	Fulgorids –	Family Fulgoridae
True Bugs	Fish-killer Bugs –	Family Belostomatidae
	Backswimmers –	Family Notonectidae
	Water Boatmen –	Family Corixidae
	Pond Skaters and Water Striders –	Families Gerridae and Veliidae
	Water Measurers –	Family Hydrometridae
	Shield Bugs –	Family Pentatomidae
	Stink Bugs, Burrowing Bugs and Ground Bugs –	Family Cydnidae
	Assassin Bugs –	Family Reduviidae
	Crusader Bugs –	Family Coreidae
	Plant Bugs –	Family Miridae
	Bark or Flat Bugs –	Family Aradidae
	Thrips –	**Order Thysanoptera**
	Alderflies and Dobsonflies –	**Order Megaloptera**
	Lacewings, Ant Lions and others –	**Order Neuroptera**
	Lacewings –	Families Chrysopidae, Hemerobiidae and others
	Mantis Flies –	Family Mantispidae

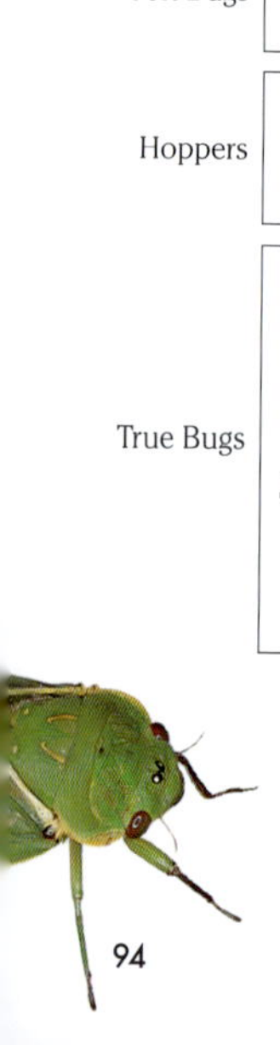

Ant Lions –	Family Myrmeleontidae
Beetles –	**Order Coleoptera**
Ground Beetles and Tiger Beetles –	Family Carabidae
Diving Beetles –	Family Dytiscidae
Whirligig Beetles –	Family Gyrinidae
Rove Beetles –	Family Staphylinidae
Passalid Beetles –	Family Passalidae
Scarabs, Dung Beetles, Chafers, Christmas Beetles –	Family Scarabaeidae
Fireflies –	Family Lampyridae
Deathwatch Beetles –	Family Anobiidae
Stag Beetles –	Family Lucanidae
Jewel Beetles –	Family Buprestidae
Darkling Beetles, Flour Beetles –	Family Tenebrionidae
Ladybird Beetles –	Family Coccinellidae
Leaf Beetles –	Family Chrysomelidae
Longicorn or Long-horned Beetles –	Family Cerambycidae
Weevils, Pinhole Borers –	Family Curculionidae
Stylopids –	**Order Strepsiptera**
Scorpion Flies, Hanging Flies –	**Order Mecoptera**
Fleas –	**Order Siphonaptera**
Flies –	**Order Diptera**
Mosquitoes –	Family Culicidae
Sandflies –	Family Ceratopogonidae
March Flies, Horse Flies –	Family Tabanidae
Robber Flies –	Family Asilidae
Fruit Flies –	Family Tephritidae
Vinegar Flies, Drosophila –	Family Drosophilidae
Houseflies, Bush Flies –	Family Muscidae
Blowflies, Bluebottles –	Family Calliphoridae
Louse Flies, Keds –	Family Hippoboscidae
Caddisflies –	**Order Trichoptera**
Moths and Butterflies –	**Order Lepidoptera**
Goat Moths –	Family Cossidae
Hawk Moths –	Family Sphingidae
Hercules Moths –	Family Saturniidae
'Army Worm' Caterpillars –	Family Noctuidae
Ulysses Butterfly and others –	Family Papilionidae
Cabbage 'Moth' –	Family Pieridae
Wasps, Sawflies, Ants and Bees –	**Order Hymenoptera**
Sawflies, Spitfires –	Families Pergidae and others
Ichneumon Wasps –	Family Ichneumonidae
Spider-hunting Wasps –	Family Pompylidae
Cuckoo Wasps –	Family Chrysididae
Velvet 'Ants' –	Family Mutilidae
Mud Dauber Wasps –	Family Sphecidae
Potter Wasps –	Families Vespidae and Eumeninae
Paper Wasps –	Families Vespidae and Polistinae
Ants –	Family Formicidae
Honey Bees, Stingless or Sugarbag Bees –	Family Apidae
Native Bees –	Families Colletidae, Halictidae, Anthophoridae and others

INDEX